700 Poetic Points

Dr. Nader F. Nowparast

Quatrain 17

Don't marry a man who is spiritually
void but has a lot of money.
Marry a man with essence who loves
you every day, rainy or sunny.
Being poor and single is more respectable
than being a man's slave.
Or being single is better than loving
a married man who is funny.

Dr. Nader F. Nowparast

700 Poetic Points

Dr. Nader F. Nowparast

Copyright © 2017 by Dr. Nader Frank Nowparast.

All rights reserved. No part of this publication may be reproduced, distributed, or transmitted in any form or by any means, including photocopying, recording, or other electronic or mechanical methods, without the prior written permission of the publisher, except in the case of brief quotations embodied in critical reviews and certain other noncommercial uses permitted by copyright law. For permission requests, write to the publisher, addressed "Attention: Permissions Coordinator," at the address below.

ARPress
45 Dan Rd., Suite 36
Canton MA 02021

Hotline: 1(800) 220-7660

Fax: 1(855) 752-6001

Ordering Information:

Quantity sales. Special discounts are available on quantity purchases by corporations, associations, and others. For details, contact the publisher at the address above.

Printed in the United States of America.

Library of Congress Control Number
ISBN-13:   Paperback   979-8-89389-040-2
                  ePub   979-8-89389-041-9

Rev. date: 03/25/2019

Acknowledgments

Hereby, I would like to express my most sincere gratitude to those who encouraged and supported me to create this English Version of 700 Poetic Points.

Among them, my beloved wife, Lili, and our precious children, Shane and Azadeh, deserve the most appreciation.

The publication of this book could not be achieved without the professional contribution made by Author Reputation Press Team.

I do hope that those Iranian children who left Iran to Western countries and do not read Farsi anymore will be able to have access to this English version of 700 Poetic Points.

Professor Nader F. Nowparast

Preface

The 700 Points that you are ready to read and enjoy are the English version of their Farsi (Persian) original version entitled 700 Guftar (points) versed and translated by Dr. Nader Frank Nowparast. The original Farsi version was published by Ketab Corporation in Los Angeles, California, in 2007. It contains seven hundred quatrains, or Rubaiyat. The first quatrain was versed when Dr. Nader F. Nowparast was seventeen years old. In addition to these quatrains, which have been his favorite poetic style, Dr. Nader F. Nowparast has versed many lyrics and elegies that have been published in Farsi magazines in Tehran and Southern California.

With the exception of fifty to sixty translated quatrains, the remaining ones were not rhymed. The rhymed translation of rhymed Farsi poetry into other languages is, indeed, severely time-consuming and, most often, impossible. Attempting to follow the Farsi rhyming rules in translating Farsi classic poetry into another language might change the concepts, meanings, and the messages expressed in its Farsi version. Although the classic Farsi poems are rhymed, but during the past half century, many famous Iranian poets have been versing rhyme-free poetry, which have been accepted and appreciated by Farsi-speaking people worldwide.

Dr. Nader F. Nowparast was born in Tehran, Iran. Prior to his arrival to the United States on a student's visa and with an American four-year academic scholarship in 1956, he wrote several short stories that were published in local magazines. But his first article in English, titled "Social Manners and Education," was published in the newsletter of Northwestern College in Alva, Oklahoma, in April 1958.

According to his academic records, Dr. Nader F. Nowparast was awarded with his BS degree at Oklahoma State University in 1961; received his MA degree in clinical psychology from the University of Tulsa, Oklahoma, in 1965; completed sixty credit units in the doctoral program in clinical psychology at the University of Texas in Austin and was awarded with a PhD degree in clinical psychology at the Florida Institute of Technology in 1980. His MA thesis was titled "An Exploratory Study of Penal Incarceration upon Personality"; his PhD dissertation had the title of "A Comparative Personality Study of Moslem, Jewish, and Christian College Students in Iran."

Dr. Nader F. Nowparast believes that poetry should be reflective of every aspect of human life—addressing, criticizing, or appraising human thoughts and behavior. Even though a quatrain is composed of two couplets, it can be regarded as a condensed summary of a book. Many of the quatrains versed by Dr. Nader F. Nowparast are reflective of human problems and criticisms of those who unjustifiably deprive others of human rights. Most of the quatrains versed by Dr. Nader F. Nowparast represent his humanitarian outlook, reality orientation, anti-sexism, and critical observations of the oppressive, dictatorial, and regressive world leaders, especially the clergies who have been governing Iran since 1979. He is genuinely against superstitions, myths, prejudices, intolerance, sexism, racism, ageism, and national (as well as international) aggression and wars. He is hopeful for world peace and wishes that world's nations will, instead of wars, use humanistic, peaceful, intelligent, international understanding and compromise strategies in resolving their differences. He asserts that according to research, close to one billion people have been killed only in wars. Dr. Nader F. Nowparast was awarded by the International Library of Poetry in 2006 for his "outstanding achievement in poetry."

As his professional records indicate, as a comprehensive mental health provider for close to forty-five years, Dr. Nader F. Nowparast began his first clinical practice as a prison psychologist at Oklahoma State Penitentiary in McAlester (1962–1963). He also functioned as the Director of Psychological Services at two youth development centers in Canonsburg and Cornwells Heights in the state of Pennsylvania (1967–1969). In addition, he provided psychometric evaluation services to Pennsylvania Department of Public Welfare and Bureau of Employment Security (1967–1969).

While in Tehran, Iran (1970–1979), Dr. Nader F. Nowparast practiced clinical psychology at Tehran University's Students' Testing and Counseling Center (1970–1973). Later, he was promoted to join the faculty of the Department of Psychiatry at Tehran University as a psychological clinician working at Roozbeh Mental Hospital (1973–1979). He is the first psychologist in Iran who ever held such a position. The two contributions that Dr. Nader F. Nowparast are very proud of are (1) his significant role in developing the first MS program in clinical psychology in Iran, offered by the Department of Psychiatry in Roozbeh Mental Hospital, and (2) developing and directing the first student counseling center in the School of Planning and Computer Application in Tehran, Iran. He also taught and provided counseling to the students.

His records also show that while in the United States (1980–present), Dr. Nader F. Nowparast provided comprehensive psychological services to hundreds of his needy fellowmen. He was licensed by the California Board of Psychology in February of 1985 after he completed only 1,500 hours of the required 3,000 hours of internship. He completed his internship hours by providing comprehensive psychological services in three outpatient clinics and in the Orange County Jail in Santa Ana, California. He was also certified as a qualified medical evaluator (QME) in 1991. And based on his previous practical experience in forensic psychology, he privately practiced clinical and forensic psychology in Orange County, California, for twenty-two years (1985–2006). He has been clinically retired since September of 2006; academically, he has been inactive since June of 2015.

As evident in his records, as an academician, Professor Nader F. Nowparast taught innumerable undergraduate and graduate courses in psychology and related fields on part-time bases. He has been academically affiliated with many colleges and universities in the United States and Iran for forty-eight years (1967–2015). While in Iran (1971–1979), he taught at the Departments of Psychology and Dentistry of the National University; at the Departments of Psychiatry, Psychology, and Business Administration of Tehran University; and at Shafa Yahyaeian Hospital, Pars College, SHMS Nursing School, Industrial School, and School of Planning and Computer Application.

While in the United States, he taught at Pennsylvania State University (1967–1969). Since his return to the United States in 1979, he taught at Newport University, where he also functioned as the dean of the School of Behavioral Sciences and an academic dean (1980–2015). He was academically affiliated with the medical school at the University of California in Irvine and the Department of Middle Eastern Studies at UCLA. He also taught at Alliant International University. In addition to teaching, Professor Nader F. Nowparast supervised close to 150 students in writing their BA research projects, MA/MS theses, and PhD dissertations in Iran and the United States. While in Iran, Professor Nader F. Nowparast was invited by and appeared on Iranian National Television to present some basic issues on child development and healthy parenting. He was the first psychologist who appeared on Iranian National Television. And as it was requested by the Iranian Ministry of Education, he presented several seminars in Kerman province of Iran, focusing on the principles and methods of student counseling. While in the United States, he also appeared on Iran Sima Television (1988–1990), presenting many issues related to mental health.

As a researcher, Dr. Nader Nowparast conducted several researches while in Tehran, Iran (1970–1979). He also conducted several researches using the psychometric data he collected on different Iranian psychiatric and nonpsychiatric samples. The instruments used in these researches were the psychological tests Dr. Nader F. Nowparast translated, for the first time, in Farsi from English. These tests included Beck Depression Inventory (BDI), Sacks and Levy Sentence Completion Test, Allport and Lindzey's Study of Values, MMPI's Mini Malt, and the Edwards Personal Preference Schedule (EPPS). He also used the Bender-Gestalt test. Among projective techniques, he gathered data by administering the Rorschach, TAT, and Draw-a-Person test. Most of the psychometric data he gathered were presented in several articles that were published in the Iranian Journal of Psychiatry in Tehran, Iran. In addition to these articles, he coauthored two books with Shukrullah Tarighati, MD, titled General Psychology and Child Psychology, which were published by the Iranian Ministry of Education Press in 1977 and 1978 respectively. The first research using the Rorschach technique in Iran was conducted by Dr. Nader F. Nowparast with the psychiatric assistance of Dr. Shukrullah Tarighati.

As a compassionate philanthropist, Dr. Nader F. Nowparast has received several certificates of appreciation for his support of several foundations and organizations, among which were the Veterans of Foreign Wars (2003–present), Disabled Veterans National Foundation (2012–present), Team USA (2014), Help Hospitalized Veterans (2015), Coalition to Salute American Heroes (2015), Paralyzed Veterans of America (2012–present), American Indian Relief Council (2014–present), American Heart Association (2014–present), United Service Organization (2013–present), Memorial Sloan Kettering Cancer Center (2014), United States Deputy Sheriffs' Association (2014), and St. Jude Children' Research Hospital (2013–2014).

Editors:

Mark A. Perez
Author Reputation Press, LLC®

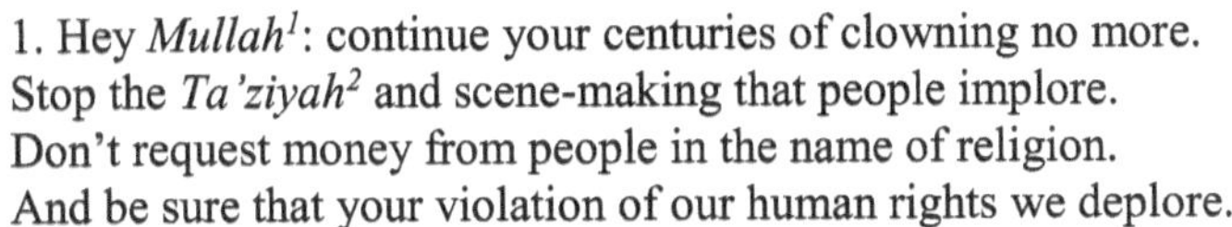

1. Hey *Mullah*[1]: continue your centuries of clowning no more.
Stop the *Ta'ziyah*[2] and scene-making that people implore.
Don't request money from people in the name of religion.
And be sure that your violation of our human rights we deplore.

2. The woman I used to love and adore.
Living without her was a painful bore.
When I thought of her with logic and lore,
She turned out to be worse than any whore.

3. Although we are human, as we firmly declare.
And of the laws of nature, we are so aware.
Even though we have mastered the sciences of war,
But of the arts of peacemaking—we are fatally unaware.

4. Hey . . . Clergies: the proofs of your claimed honesty—we have never seen.
In your sermons are hidden deceptions so stupid, misleading and mean.
Don't distort the true verses of Holy Books no more, because.
We don't trust you, and your sermons are not worth a bean.

1: *Mullah* = *Sheikh* = *Akhound*: A Moslem clergyman equivalent to a preacher, priest or rabbi.

2: *Ta'ziyah*: A theatrical passion play in remembrance of the tragic Massacre of Imam Hussein, his family and followers by the troop of Yazid ibn Mu'awiyah (Caliph) in Karbela (680 AD). Imam Husein was the second son of Imam Ali (601-66 AD) who was Prophet Muhammad's cousin and son-in-law. Imam Husein was Imam Ali's first son; he was poisoned by his Sunni opponents. Masoummah-Zahra was the daughter of Prophet Muhammad. She was the mother of Imam Hassan and Imam Hussein. Imam 'Ali and Khadijah (Prophet Muhammad's first wife) were the first two persons who accepted Islam. Prophet Muhammad had nine to thirteen wives, of whom the youngest was Ayasheh, who was nine years old and the daughter of Abu Bakr (First Caliph). Prophet Muhammad was also the father-in-law of 'Uthman (Third Caliph) who gathered Muhammad's revelations in the form of Quran. 'Uthman married two daughters of Prophet Muhammad. Prophet Muhammad's three sons died at an early age.

5. My beloved: With your exception, my other desires have left my heart.
My soul moans because we are so frequently apart.
But my searching, tearful and eager eyes,
Will be restlessly looking for you in every mart.

6. Get up, come on, and let us leave this bondage to its pest.
Leave its wealth, blasphemy, faiths, myths, and the rest.
Then, free from what is and is not, and the past and future.
With our love and serenity, build for ourselves a peaceful nest.

7. Oh . . . You Obese Mullah who sound like a mule.
Have you lost your mind or you have become a fool?
Don't disturb my sleep with your screaming and braying.
Come down from the minaret; be quiet and cool.

8. What would happen if you were mine?
And you were in my life's cup like wine?
What would happen if we were engaged?
And you, as the sun of my life, did always shine?

9. Oh . . . Iranians: wake up from the dream of ignorance.
And motivate your hidden potentials for scientific excellence.
If you desire to rise above others and be happy forever,
Always abstain from mullahs' superstitions and scientific negligence.

10. The pretty and unhappy woman who had no lover or friend,
She always read the *Holy Books*[3] and to nothing else she did attend.
Last night after her lips became acquainted with a cup of wine,
Her body got hungry for hugs and her lips for kisses with no end.

---

*3: **Holy Books**: Old and New Testaments.

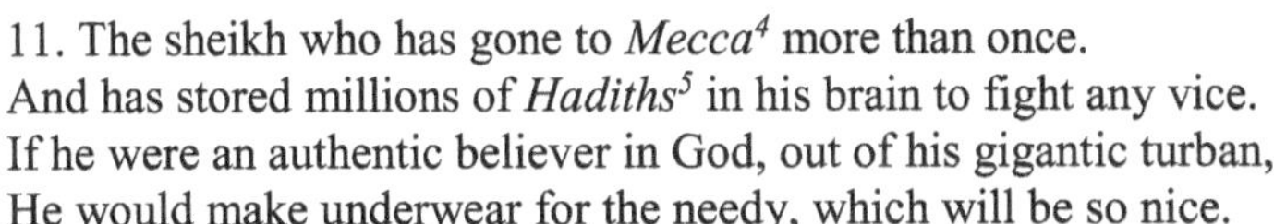

11. The sheikh who has gone to *Mecca*[4] more than once.
And has stored millions of *Hadiths*[5] in his brain to fight any vice.
If he were an authentic believer in God, out of his gigantic turban,
He would make underwear for the needy, which will be so nice.

12. I and my beloved were sipping wine and humming in moonlight.
The beauty of rose garden with the candle and butterfly was out of sight.
While free of life's worries, I was full of mirth and had fun.
Suddenly the death angel showed up, and while sneering, he said: "All right."

13. About faith and blasphemy, how long more should we hear?
Between doubts and certainty, how long we must change our mind's gear?
Of the bumpy road of life, only a short trail is left.
For how long should we listen to the truth and false, my dear?

14. When the sun sets, the thoughts of you rush into my mind.
When the sun rises, I look for you but no trace of you I find.
Even though my soul is constantly searching for you, but using my logic.
I am gradually realizing that you are neither good for me nor my kind.

15. The girl I loved, and for whom I did care and long,
She loved me too and wrote me a lot of love song.
Alas, by the force of her parents, unwilling and depressed,
She married her cousin, who took her to Hong Kong.

16. Do you know how you came into existence as a man, not as a brute?
And out of nothing, into flesh and blood, you did spread your root.
Two tiny particles out of love met and planted your seeds.
And with no choice or awareness, you blossomed as their fruit.

---

4 Mecca: A city in Saudi Arabia, where the home of God is located. It was first built by Adam (God's first apostle) and later by Prophet Ibrahim. Every Moslem should visit Mecca at least once in their lifetime. While praying, Moslems should face it; the body of the dead should be buried facing the Mecca.

5 Hadiths: Narrations of the deeds and words of Prophet Muhammad and his Descendants.

17. Don't marry a man who is spiritually void but has a lot of money.
Marry a man with essence who loves you every day, rainy or sunny.
Being poor and single is more respectable than being a man's slave.
Or being single is better than loving a married man who is funny.

18. The mullah who asserts it is religiously sinful to drink wine
And claims his chastity is in the halo around his head that does shine.
He has three legal wives, but every night through temporary marriage,
He deflowers an under-aged girl, drinks vodka, and goes out of line.

19. I hope one of these nights our lips meet, with yours atop.
They will help us to reap our romantic crop.
And while I tenderly kiss every spot of your body,
Once or twice, I will kiss the lip of the wine's cup.

20. Oh . . .You Girl: you are lovely, desirable and full of coyness.
But because you dislike dancing and playing or hearing poetry, you are joyless.
Which sin have you committed, or which God's law have you violated
That you are praying every day and night asking for God's forgiveness?

21. God has blended the fragrance of jasmine in your clay.
He has coded your beautiful body with silver ray.
Since he has endowed your lips with honey, my dear,
I don't eat honey anymore, and for it I don't have to pay.

22. My friends: I wish there were hell and paradise.
And for our deeds, there will be penalty and price.
Mullah: I hope you with your evil colleagues will be in hell.
And the heaven will be cleansed of your satanic vice.

23. Oh . . . My Dear Ladies: why do you listen to and get sad by the sexist?
Don't forget your worth; without you no one will be born to exist.
If you sharpen your intelligence and use it, without a doubt,
The mullahs' baseless prejudice against you will never persist.

24. Hey . . . Mullahs: I am bored with your wire-pulling and intrigue.
Of your chronic ignorance and bragging, my soul feels fatigue.
I am surprised, why in the progressive current Atomic Age,
The depth of ignorance increases in you and your league.

25. Hey . . . You Man, who go somewhere every night,
You are the one who is disloyal; don't pick up a fight.
If you want your wife remain loyal to you,
Be loyal to her, and into real love gain some insight.

26. Alas, in gaining your love, I lost my sense of youth.
My bright days felt dark and did not anymore sooth.
My heart that was pure like a flower became polluted
With the impurities of your love, which was so uncouth.

27. Hey . . . You Woman: you are more sinful and filthy than the devil.
You are more deceitful than the demon, in action and will.
Stop fornication and neglecting your children.
You are more evil than all the whores in *Newville*[6].

28. Oh . . . Neighboring Girl: I beg you, please come by
And give me a kiss as a gift, don't be sad and shy.
If the tulip does not show up in winter, it is justified.
But it is *Norooz*[7] now, come to me and don't make an alibi.

---

6 Newville: New City (Shahre Noe in Farsi): A section of the southern part of Tehran, Iran,
where many houses of prostitution are/were located.

7 Norooz: Iranian New Year celebrated on the twenty-first of March (first day of spring) of
each year.

29. If you really and always think of God faithfully
And build your life on what the *Quran*[8] says, thankfully.
Where God has said in Quran that in the month of *Muharram*[9]
Beat your chest with chains, shed tears, and scream painfully?

30. Hey . . . Dear Ladies: for nobody, you ever become slaves.
Wake up, and strive for the rights you deserve and crave.
In all societies your rights should be equal to those of men.
Don't stop until you obtain your rights, enhance them and save.

31. People, who against drinking alcohol, collect document
And about it, with non-Moslems have hostile argument.
With the sinful profits they make from dividend and forestalling,
They go to *Hajj*[10] in order to meet Islamic requirement.

32. Oh . . . God: don't make me feel fed up with life's pain, my master.
With sickness and anguish don't afflict my beloved, Aster.
I will gladly accept any calamity you may bring me,
But please protect her from misery, sorrows and disaster.

33. The more beautiful a woman is, the more unwise she might be.
She might be even more uninformed about the world than a baby.
When she loses her beauties, her intelligence will emerge.
But then, she will be very depressed and hopeless, maybe.

34. Oh . . . My Friend: why you are so tearful at each night and every morning
And in the month of Muharram you hurt yourself while bleeding and burning?
If Imam Hussein was murdered in Karbela and became a martyr,
Why for him in the land of Persia (Iran), you are mourning?

8: Quran: Moslems' Holy Book; God sent its content to Muhammad through Gabriel, the Archangel.

9: Muharram: An Arabic month during which Imam Hussein, his family, and companions were deprived of water and murdered by the troops of Yazid ibn Mu'awiyah, the Caliph.

10: Hajj: A pillar of Islam mandating every Moslem to take pilgrimage to Mecca once in their lifetime.

35. Hey . . . Mullah: it is none of your business, if I am sad and drink.
It is none of your business, if with your followers I don't link.
I am thirsty for realities but your heaven is a mythical mirage.
It is none of your business, if of your pious deeds, I don't even think.

36. Happy are those who follow our creed and feel no hate.
They eat bread and dates, and have poetry, wine and a true soul mate.
The people who have vain and foolish restraints around their existence,
Embitter the sweetness of their lives like a chained inmate.

37. I madly love your coquettish manners, you hear?
I adore the gorgeous content of your brassiere.
Come under the weeping willow tree tonight
So I will kiss your sugar-sweet lips, my dear.

38. Hey . . . Mullah: it is none of your business, if I am sinful
Or I drink wine, and love a girl who is beautiful.
Don't criticize me, if I read the books of *Darwin*[11] and *Hegel*[12],
Or I ask God many questions, to whom I am thankful.

39. Hey . . . Mullah: do you want the wealth of entire world for your own?
And have the best things of life at your home to be shown?
If egotism and narcissism are the religious values you promote,
I have no religion; you keep this animalistic religion in your zone.

40. Oh . . . My Mother: for me, you have been more precious than a crown.
In front of my father's wisdom and civilities, I will always bow down.
Although I am now twenty years old, of the secrets of the world,
I am much more aware than the chief mullah in this town.

11: *Charles Darwin (1809-1882):* British naturalist who developed the theory of human evolution.

12: *George Hegel (1770-1831):* German philosopher, physician, and writer.

41. Hey . . . Akhounds: you are impure in soul, and filthy from head to toe.
You are shameless and dishonest in the eyes of friend and foe.
Your long and bushy beard is the symbol of your deceitfulness.
Get rid of it with *Vaujebee¹³*; shave it or mow.

42. Hey . . . You Girl: you have gorgeous figure and beautiful look.
Remember last night, of my lips, how many kisses you took?
Why now that it is time for lovemaking, you are superstitiously.
Making an augury, counting the beads, and consulting a book?

43. You are my idol and except you I worship no one.
I am addicted to you, and will not give up such a fun.
I swear to God: I envy no body or anything
Except the dresses you have on every day and night.

44. About you my love, I have with my heart, many discussions.
With my mind about you, I have many argumentative sessions.
About every spot in your body, from head to toe,
You don't believe how many desires I have as romantic missions.

45. Hey . . . You Girl who pressed my chest against yours so tight
And kissed my lips many times after you turned off the light,
Why you broke your promise, and did not take your pills?
So, as you promised me, we could get romantic tonight?

46. My sadness is the effect of your mystic romance.
My withering is the effect of your lovely eyes and glance.
My hopelessness is due to your painful negligence.
And my insanity is due to your childish ignorance.

47. Oh . . . God: make my romance competitor forever miserable.
Make him forever debased and passionately incapable.
Let a king cobra bite and poison him to death.
Or let a gang of wolves tear him into pieces eatable.

13: Vaujebee: A cream which was and is used in Iran to remove the pubic hair.

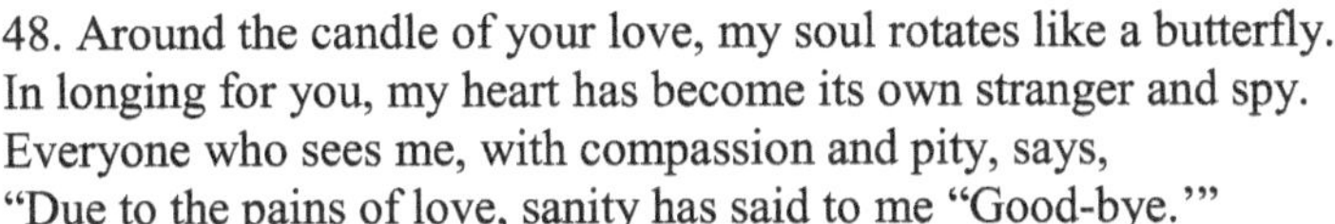

48. Around the candle of your love, my soul rotates like a butterfly.
In longing for you, my heart has become its own stranger and spy.
Everyone who sees me, with compassion and pity, says,
"Due to the pains of love, sanity has said to me "Good-bye.'"

49. I saw a little blister on the smiling lip of my beloved, Miss——
I love her beautiful teeth, and smiling lips which I always miss.
She asked me flirtatiously, what would its remedy be?
I said: My kiss my dear, my kiss my dear, my kiss.

50. The elderly who spent their youth playing sinful games,
And they turned their back toward God, and did what a heretic aims.
Now, afraid of death, God's revenge, and fires of hell.
They are faithful now and cry out: "God is great" with no shames.

51. Oh . . . God: please have mercy on my soul which is now torn.
My beloved is the only asset I have had since I was born.
Make me blind, mute, deaf, and break both of my legs.
But please, don't let her foot get hurt by a thorn.

52. My Darling: since my heart is not satisfied with our romance
For separating my lips from the wine cup, there is no chance.
The wine bottle is empty now, and my patience has exhausted.
Thus, in taming my heart with wine and prayers, there would be no advance.

53. Oh . . . My Friend: don't laugh at my sorrowful mood.
Don't sadden my heart by being so rude.
The rotating world has trapped me in this condition.
Don't ever rely on the rotating world, which is no good.

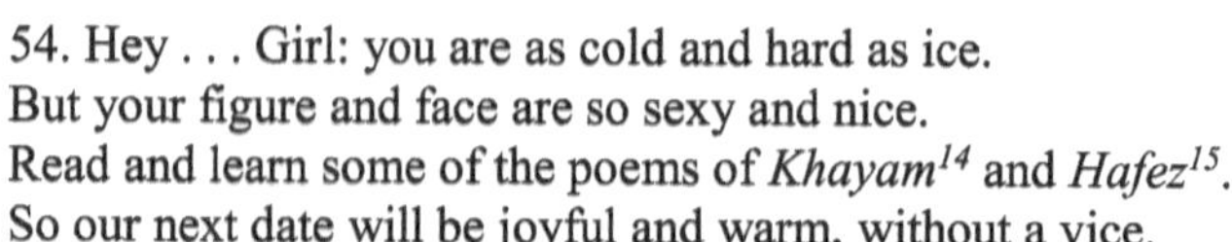

54. Hey . . . Girl: you are as cold and hard as ice.
But your figure and face are so sexy and nice.
Read and learn some of the poems of *Khayam*[14] and *Hafez*[15].
So our next date will be joyful and warm, without a vice.

55. Tell me you girl: why you are so sad.
Why like a thorn, you sting my soul and make me so mad?
I have always given you sympathy and affection.
Why you never sympathize with me and make me glad?

56. I saw a girl in a church who had beautiful curves and edges.
She was delicate, blond and angelic with beautiful design.
She winked at me and whispered in my ear, and said,
"In Christianity, having a *Sighah*[16] without recitation is just fine."

57. A sheikh told her son: "Drink wine no more.
You are ignorant of God and religion, what for?"
The son replied: "I would stop drinking provided
You burn your turban and shave your beard; you are a bore."

58. Hey . . . You Girl who has long blond hair
And your blue and beautiful eyes are much better than fair,
Don't open your blossom-looking mouth, because
Your tongue and the stings of bees have a lot to share.

59. Oh . . . Our King: fear God and don't fight him.
And don't deceive us with your sweet talks.
Don't buy weapons; we are not in a war.
Don't fill up the West's pockets with our wealth.

14: Omar Khayyam (1048-1131 AD): An Iranian mathematician, astronomer, poet and philosopher. His Ruba'iyat (Quatrains) have been translated into more than fifty languages.

15: Hafiz (1325-1389 AD): An Iranian legendary philosopher and mystic poet.

16: Sighah: Islamic temporary marriages, lasting from minutes to years. The man or the woman should recite some Arabic verse from Quran before they get intimate. In Islam, a man can have four legal wives and at least four Sighahs or Concubines (in Nisa Chapter, Quran).

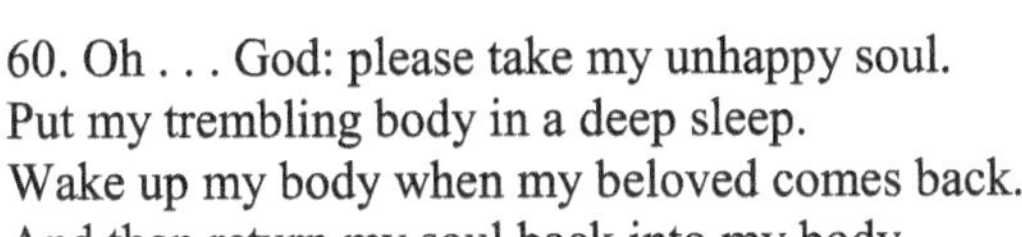

60. Oh . . . God: please take my unhappy soul.
Put my trembling body in a deep sleep.
Wake up my body when my beloved comes back.
And then return my soul back into my body.

61. Hey . . . You, who are so proud of your wealth, looks and youth.
And have fame, high status and glory, but deny the truth.
Don't debase those whose statuses are lower than yours.
You are ignorant and insolent, doomed to die, so uncouth.

62. Oh . . . My heart: you will finally kill me with anguish.
You will make me insane and slit-chest with no wish
With all the unfulfilled wishes I have now in my youth,
You finally put me in a grave, after I will perish.

63. People ask me: "Why" I "moan all day and night?"
"And why" I am "so sad and tearful lacking delight?"
I tell them: "My beloved left saying she will be back next week.
But a year has passed, but no news of her is in sight."

64. Hey . . . Nader: why you are so unhappy and heart sore?
Don't be so sad because your beloved is sometimes a bore.
Be happy and appreciate life because in the promised paradise, you will be
Cheated and sorry because there will be no music and library, for sure.

65. Last night my eyes shed blood for your sorrows.
Even my enemy felt sorry and upset for me.
I decided to drink wine to decrease my sadness and tears.
But the bottle was empty, so my tears and grief became worst.

66. She drank wine, got half-drunk, and fell asleep on the lap of mine.
My desire for making love with her was about to make me to go out of line.
When I stole a kiss from her beautiful and expecting lips,
She quickly woke up and said: "Blessed be the wine."

67. While in a tavern, I heard my friend saying,
"This one-colored wine is better than a multifaced beloved.
And whoever makes me happy like this wine.
I will award her with my faith, heart, and wealth."

68. I became romantically involved with a girl.
With her love I became free of my sorrows.
One night she left this world, and forty days
I visited her gravesite with sadness and grieve.

69. Last night she gave me a cold and unkind look.
With her stinging tongue—she rejected and saddened me.
But after she compared me with her lewd and abusive lover,
She felt sorry, and asked: "How" I am "doing?"

70. Hey . . . You, who created the World,
I have two questions, with two hundred greetings and gratitude.
You are our creator, and we are your creatures,
But who was your creator, and by whom was he created?

71. Oh . . . My Heart: for how long you are sad and in pain?
How long you are sorry because my beloved is not wise?
While young, I feel old and disappointed because
You my heart: are groaning due to lack of true love.

72. Do you know why the mullahs are brutal?
And in forbidding the wine, they become fierce and rigid?
Because they are afraid if they drink wine, they will see
The truth and realities, and might become sorry and shameful.

73. I am the one who is kind to people, but receive no kindness.
I speak nicely with others but they talk to me with bitterness.
I shed tears for grieves of friends and foes.
But for my tears and sorrows, I receive carelessness.

74. Without you my beloved, my life passes by fast with sorrows.
And my bright mornings pass like dark nights.
In your absence, I feel like every moment of my life
Is a day long, during which my soul leaves my body.

75. Hey . . . You Girl who have the fragrance of jasmine,
Why do you keep fruitlessly flirting with me?
Even though you are good-looking and have a nice figure,
But toward you, I have no feelings and attraction.

76. No one will lovingly bow down before you like me, my dear lady.
No one will devote his soul for your admirable qualities my dear.
But be aware: When you become aged and ugly.
Even the loose dog on the street will not look at you.

77. Oh . . . My Beloved: without you my soul is not free of sadness.
My heart will not calm down with advice and reasoning.
The pains and sorrows of lovers disappear with wine.
But my anguishes will not go away with the help of wine.

78. The beloved girl, of whom the beauty of spring was envious.
And like me, more than hundred men desired for her kisses.
Yesterday I saw her in the bosom of her grave.
Where, the dust was kissing her lips constantly.

79. Hey . . .You Deceitful Akhound: leash up your mouth.
Don't tamper with everything we do and say.
In doomsday: God, I and Satan, in your absence
With logic and rationality will get along fine.

80. They tell me "drinking wine will reap evil."
"Love and poetry result in heresy and sinfulness."
"Don't fall in love, don't drink, and don't poetize."
Then, what will encourage me to enjoy living?

81. I had a lot of nostalgia and loneliness last night.
I dated a girl who was beautiful but not very bright.
When I drank wine all of my sorrows left my heart, except the sadnessof
Missing my family and country, which were both out of sight.

82. People who suffer in the month of Muharram with grief and pain,
And for hours they beat their nude chest with chain.
Even though they, apparently, shed tears for Imam Hussein,
In reality, however, for their own miseries they shed tears like rain.

83. Hey . . . My Sighs: love has arrived, so make a nest in my chest.
Hey . . . My Tears: come on since my eyes are your natural nest.
Hey . . . Happiness: go away because my heart has no room for you.
Hey . . . Sadness: come on, my heart is your home at best.

84. Hey . . . My Friends and Country-Loving Iranians,
Sacrifice yourself only for your country and countrymen.
And instead of saying: God, king, and nation up to now.
Keep saying: God, country, and countrymen from now on.

85. Hey . . . Dear Ladies: it is not the time to be intelligently sluggish,
Nor it is the time for being silent and covering up the truth.
If you thinks of Sighah (concubine) even with its Islamic justification,
It is not, at all, different from selling oneself as a harlot.

86. I am thirty year old now, and seeking the secrets of mind.
Iran is my country, and my birthplace is Tehran.
On 22nd of August in nineteen hundred and thirty-one,
I arrived into this world with no choice and awareness.

87. If you are looking for your origin my friend,
You are neither made of dust or the rotation of galaxies.
Contrary to superstitions, and based on scientific facts,
You, like other animals, have originated from the ocean.

88. Hey . . . You Clean-Hearted people: don't be deceived by the preachers.
Don't be betrayed by what they say or what they wear.
Don't be saddened by the bitterness of the truth and reality.
Even if the preacher's deceptive talk may sound sweet, don't accept it.

89. Come on you girl, please don't think of me anymore.
Throw me out of your heart, what are you sad for?
The differences between us are innumerable.
Forget and forgive me; you can find a more compatible man; I am sure.

90. Hey . . . You Girl: don't refill my wine cup.
Don't ask me for the address of my jeweler's shop.
When I am ready to get married,
I will select my bride out of Iranian girls; so stop.

91. I am lonely and sad in fighting with my heart.
I have no confidence, no wine and no music.
I'm away from my home country; no news from friends and foes.
Oh . . . God: when I will be leaving this land to go home?

92. Hey . . . You beautiful blond classmate,
You are truly gorgeous in figure and eyes.
I told you several times don't call me anymore.
I will not give my heart to a loose woman.

93. Whether you are gratified or dissatisfied in life,
And whether you are famous or have no fame,
The Death Angel has put a trap on your way,
And one day, you will finally fall in it.

94. Hey . . . You Girl who shared my books,
Why don't you respond to my calls?
From the day I have come to America,
You have been always the only guest in my dreams.

95. Oh . . . God: be sure that man will never become angel-hearted.
He will not be afraid of your punishment and anger.
With your Holy Verses, threats of hell, and promises of heaven,
He will never become a real human, despite your wishes.

96. Last night my sight, stealthily, from her neck,
Slipped down into her cleavage.
I told it "Don't go further," but it went and from her nipples,
It trembled and fell down in her tender lap.

97. Oh . . . You Girl who are my Classmate,
It is wise if I cut down my contact with you.
I am afraid of not passing this course
If I let you attract all of my attention.

98. Hey . . . You Girl: you have a lot of coyness,
And your eyes are blue and beautiful.
From your lack of wisdom it is clear, however, that
Instead of human brain, you have the brain of a duck.

99. Happy are those whose freedom is protected by their wisdom,
And their intelligence and hearts are their genuine advisers.
The fortunate is the one who in his journey to nonexistence
His load of happiness is much heavier than his load of sorrows.

100. Oh . . . You, the Essence of My Soul: are you my beloved or not?
Please tell me: can we try to be more compatible or not?
Life goes on even without our romance.
Are you going to be still in my heart or not?

101. Hey . . . You Girl: where were you in my absence?
Why did you buy wine and put it on my tab?
If drinking wine is prohibited in your religion,
Why did you drink my wine with a blasphemous?

102. Oh . . . My Friend: Avoid irrational guilt feeling.
Don't find sanctuary in a bar because you are guilt-ridden.
Be happy, and make your friends and foes happy.
Don't ever hurt animals and plants.

103. I hope you never get tied up with the cowards
And you will never be kept in prison unjustly.
I do hope that if you are eager to fall in love,
You will never fall in love with ignorant beloved.

104. Oh . . . My Dear Lady: I will fascinate you with my accomplishments,
And I will entice you with my niceties and poeticism.
But if you get fat, become stupid, or get lazy and insipid,
I will kick you out of my heart, and throw you out of my mind.

105. Oh . . . My Friends: don't ask the Akhounds about scientific information.
Don't expect light from a bulb if it is not connected to electric power.
As long as Akhounds are drowned in the marsh of superstitions,
Don't expect their level of stupidity will go down.

106. It is winter and the chilliness is intolerable.
Being with you, however, I feel the warmth of your love.
Come and sit down; tell me what I can get you,
Something sweet and warm or some wine?

107. Oh . . . You: the ointment of my grief, don't forget your promises.
Don't listen to the meaningless promises of the vile people.
The lion of my heart is eager to be caught by your lasso.
Don't waste your time in hunting a rabbit-natured man.

108. With the exception of your love, I have nothing in my heart.
But expect tribulation, I have no harvest of loving you.
I have resolved the problems of hundreds friends and foes.
And except you, I have problems with no one.

109. Hey . . . Dear Girl: I have not heard from you four years.
I don't know if you are alive or you have passes away.
If you are alive please send me a message.
If you left this world, please appear in my dreams.

110. They tell me my "beloved is not a Moslem because
She does not believe in heaven, its *Houris*[17] and *Ghelmaans*[18]."
I tell them: "Whether she worships an idol or God,
In the faith of love, there is no blasphemy and religiosity."

111. Hey . . . Mullah: why do you get upset about what I say?
How long you want to avoid facing the truth?
If for few years, I have been mildly influenced by the West,
You have been under the influence of Arabs for fourteen centuries.

112. I met a beautiful Christian young lady in the church
To which she donated a lot of her own money.
In expressing my gratitude, I asked her if I could kiss her.
She said: "Of course, if you join our congregation."

113. Hey . . . You Gorgeous and well-mannered girl,
I see your eyes asking me who am I.
My name is Nader, and I am from Persia (Iran).
What is your name? And where do you come from?

114. Oh. . . My Friends: don't intent to fight your enemy.
Don't reveal your secrets to your foes.
Instead of hurting your enemy, treat him with peacefulness.
And don't awaken the snake which is asleep.

17: Houris: 70 (?) fourteen-year-old virgin girls in paradise who provide full service to male martyrs, who were killed or committed suicide in defense of Islam and God, and all male residents of heaven.

18: Ghelmaans: 70 (?) fourteen-year-old virgin males in heaven, who provide full service to female martyrs, who were killed or committed suicide in defense of Islam and God, and all female residents of heaven.

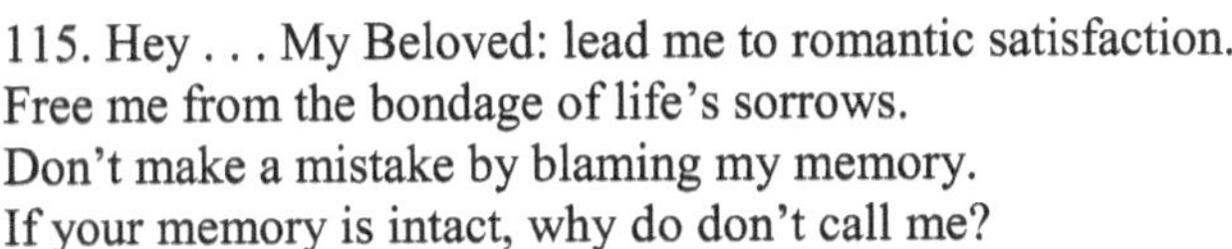

115. Hey . . . My Beloved: lead me to romantic satisfaction.
Free me from the bondage of life's sorrows.
Don't make a mistake by blaming my memory.
If your memory is intact, why do don't call me?

116. Hey . . . You Mullah: Your temper is like tiger's.
You look like a gigantic whale.
From your conduct and sermons, it is clear that
You are either insane or under the influence of drugs.

117. Oh . . . Iran: It is impossible to completely describe your sorrows.
Your problems can't be summarized even in two hundred books.
You will never pick up a flower from the garden of sciences
Unless you totally eliminate the parasites of superstitions.

118. Oh . . . You Girl who are Cuddly and have a Nice Figure,
I don't want you to kiss me repeatedly.
Even though, I like you very much.
But I have no intention to get married.

119. Hey . . . You Girl: who are gorgeously figured and are beautiful,
And you claim to be a genuine follower of Jesus,
Shame on you; do not bother me anymore.
Why you are so loose and impudent in your thoughts and actions?

120. In the rotation of the galaxies I see good and evil.
In the operation of the world I see permanent flaws
Even though we know God is completely perfect.
But in the creation of human, I see three hundred mistakes.

121. The sheikh who totally follows the God
And prays to God and reads Quran from dawn to night,
Every moment he fabricates a narration for his own benefit,
And by doing so, he insults the Prophet and Islam.

122. Oh . . . God: once in a while pay me a little attention.
Send me a beloved and decrease my tension.
Create another Layla or another *Shirin*[19].
Make me like *Majun and Farhad*[20] as a pension.

123. Oh . . . God: I am indisposed; give me a chance to travel.
I am bored with people I know; send me a stranger.
I got no benefits from the daughters of Eve.
Oh . . . You the daughter of grapes (wine): help me if you can.

124. Oh . . . God: You should not have taken the girl I loved.
Why did you take her at the age of twenty-five?
If you had planned to take her away from me forever,
Why did you let me to truly fall in love with her?

125. Before you get impatient and angry, my friend,
And use abusive language or become dangerous,
You better have a consultation session with Nader.
Otherwise, you will suffer depressive guilt from your mistake.

126. Hey . . . You Girl who has a pretty face
And you have desirable lips and figure.
Do you have a *snake's bead*[21]?
That thousands of men are infatuated with you?

127. The woman who had a lot of grievances from her husband,
And in his absence, she negatively criticized him publically.
I saw her at his burial site; while shedding tears she was
Telling the mourners how nice and respectful her husband was.

19: Layla and Shirin: In Iranian literature, they are female beloved; analogous to Juliet.

20: Majnun and Farhad: In Iranian literature, they are male lovers; analogous to Romeo.

21: Snake's Bead: Mohreh (Bead) of Mar (Snake): An Iranian adage indicating that whoever has a piece of snake's spinal cord, is mysteriously adored, loved, and admired by many people.

128. Oh . . . You Girl: in the creative artistry of God, you are a masterpiece.
In the season of winter, you look like spring.
There is no doubt that you are gorgeous all over.
Now tell me what wisdom have you stored in your brain?

129. Hey . . . You Moslems: why do you believe in superstitions?
Why you are hatefully against *Fredrick Niche*[22]?
The non-Moslems have been conquering the galaxies,
But you are still lost in the curves of uncertainty and illusions.

130. Do you know why I don't like the West?
Who benefits from the wars between the nations that don't make weapons?
It first creates animosity between two shahs or national leaders
And then sells to them expensive armaments.

131. Oh . . . You Girl: I'm sad because our intimacy did not come around.
You are gorgeous, but lack sincerity.
I know: No one has ever been born from her/his mother
Hundred per cent perfect in body and soul.

132. Hey . . . You Girl: I know your father is a preacher.
Once in a while your conduct makes me unhappy.
Even though you are glamorous and desirable,
But in spite of your sweet lips, you tongue is full of stings.

133. Hey . . . Iranians: don't ever say your problems will not be resolved.
Your problems will not be solved with grief, prayers and opium or alcohol.
Your will never find solutions to your problems, unless
The theocratic and dictatorial Mullahs are completely out of government.

22: *Fredrick Niche (1844-1900)*: German rationalistic philosopher. He authored a book titled What Did Zoroaster Say? Zoroaster was the first founder of monotheism, and his teachings inspired the rise of Judaism, Christianity, and Islam. Zoroastrianism was the religion in Persia (Iran) prior to Arab invasion (642-65 AD) while Omar was the Third Caliph.

134. Except you my dear, I don't have a beloved.
How many times I have told you so?
If you are in love with someone else,
Let me know, so I can search for a beloved.

135. Do you know why I keep praying to the galaxies,
And with tearful eyes, I have craving for wine?
I am trying, with the aid of wine, tears and God
Push your image out of my heart.

136. Oh . . . Life: I will not lean on you tightly.
I will not build a house on the running water.
Oh . . . Shah you better know: as long as blood runs in my veins,
I will never bow my head or body down before you.

137. When I sleep, I will see your lips, eyes, face and figure in my dreams.
When I am awake, I eagerly long and search for you.
On the day of resurrection, if my soul returns back into my body,
I will get out of my grave and anxiously search for you.

138. Hey . . . You Mullah: you are an imposter with rotten beliefs.
You have made religion shameful and painful for your own benefits.
Why do you expect me to confirm what you preach by saying Amen?
Your sermons are stupid, nonsensical and misleading.

139. Hey . . . Our Shah: don't try to make us happy with your promises.
Promise with no action yields no benefits.
With our rich oil, you have not been able to solve our problems.
How you are going to solve our problems if we run out of it?

140. The mullah, who is seriously against drinking and fornication
And claims he will ignore this world for the sake of God,
Every night he sleeps with a new concubine (temporary wife)
And drinks wine "as medicine."

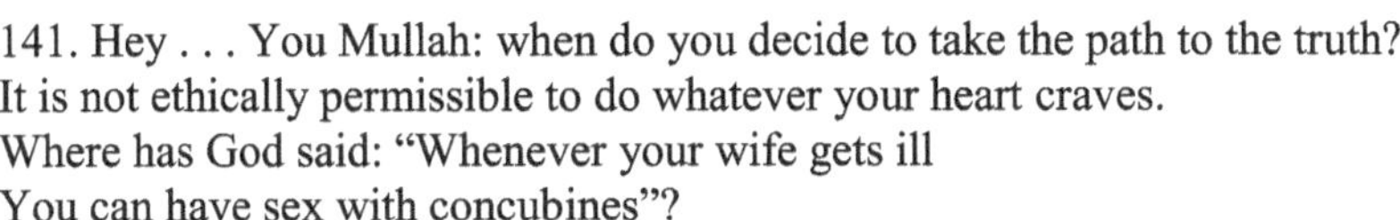

141. Hey . . . You Mullah: when do you decide to take the path to the truth?
It is not ethically permissible to do whatever your heart craves.
Where has God said: "Whenever your wife gets ill
You can have sex with concubines"?

142. For some time, I moaned of the sorrows of love.
For some time, I appreciated wine, poetry and knowledge.
Realize how fast our lives pass by.
Suddenly, as fast as a blink, I realized I am forty years old.

143. Hey . . . Shah: why we are forced to revere you?
We always have criticized you for your egotism.
Why should we be forced to bow down
In front of your portrait on your birthdays?

144. Hey . . . You Mullah: for how long you talk nonsense?
For how long you gossip about your spouse?
Even though God is not a carpenter,
He has nicely matched you two with one another.

145. Oh . . . My Dear Friends: don't sadden others with your vengeance
Compromise with your friends and don't hurt your enemies.
In dealing with people and the affairs of the world,
Don't deny or give up your human rights.

146. I have seen many flowers where the cacti grow.
I know many enlightened people in the bondage of darkness.
I have seen many intelligent people residing in insane asylum,
And I have seen many insane people who are out of mental hospitals.

147. Don't belittle your worth by bending your head.
Of the table of life, try to get your share of bread.
If you expect others to genuinely respect you.
You better have respect for yourself, alive or dead.

148. Hey . . . You who drink the ignorance the mullahs poured in your cup of life,
Your lack of wisdom provides mullah's best satisfaction and benefits.
If you don't use your intelligence and sharpen your sword of wisdom,
You could never free yourself and your country from mullah's bondage.

149. Do you know why you are not called a jewel?
And your age is reaching fifty but you are not married yet?
Even though your face, hair, and figure are beautiful,
You are bad-tempered, bossy and have no essence.

150. Hey . . . You Akhounds: you have lost your modesty.
Don't imitate dogs' temper and barking.
Based on what you think and talk, it is evident that
You have not been taking your prescribed medication.

151. At these cold, cloudy and starless nights
During which I teach the truth in classes but not at the pulpit.
It is only the hope of being with you my dear *Lili*[23].
That gives my heart the sparks of warmth and happiness.

152. Hey . . . You Sheikhs: misleading the people is not teaching the true faith.
With what authority you are denying the truth?
Oblations, *Dakheel*[24] and the verses of Holy Quran,
Never decrease the symptoms of or treat an illness.

153. Hey . . . Our Shah: the King of kings: I have a question for you.
With the exception of being speechless, what are my options?
With the existence of *SAVAK*[25] that obeys your orders,
What opportunity do I have to tell the truth?

23: Lili: My wife's first name.

24: Dakheel: To tie up a piece of fabric around the wall or fence of the graves of Imams.

25: SAVAK: Iranian National Security and Information Organization.

154. Hey . . . You Mullahs: If tavern is my temple, it is not your business.
Whatever I planted in my garden of life, it is not your business.
You better be concerned about your own place after life.
Whether I go to heaven or hell, it is not your business.

155. The sheikh who is a pimp and matchmaker.
And he is filthy-minded, stupid and vulgar.
He has been mentally sick with pedophilia, because
He has temporarily married a girl who is ten years old.

156. *Masoummah*[26] who was only nine years old.
And she was forced by her parents to marry a sexist sheikh.
The day after their marriage was consummated
She felt so abused and depressed, that she killed herself.

157. The ignorant hajji who was our neighbor.
And people were surprised of his spiritual purity.
While drunk, he murdered his son.
And when he became alert he said: "God gave and God took,"

158. Hey . . . You Akhounds: Satan is more compassionate than you are.
The heretic's thoughts are more realistic than yours.
There are billions of non-Moslems in the world
Who are much more peaceful than you will ever be.

159. Without sorrow, happiness cannot be recognized.
Your load of concerns will be heavier if you are in love.
The criterion of sadness is mirth only.
Measuring happiness is impossible without sadness.

26: Masoummah: Female name in Arabic/Iranian languages.

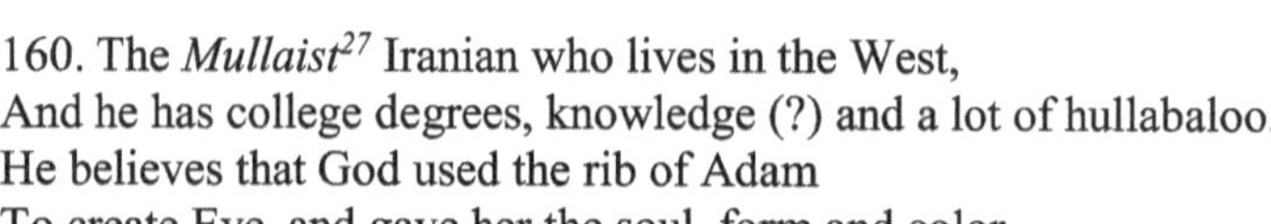

160. The *Mullaist*[27] Iranian who lives in the West,
And he has college degrees, knowledge (?) and a lot of hullabaloo.
He believes that God used the rib of Adam
To create Eve, and gave her the soul, form and color.

161. Hey . . . You Mullahs: you are, indeed, ignorant, debased and crazy.
You are the ones who have always degraded and abused women.
Don't justify your animalistic sexuality with frequent temporary marriages.
You are, indeed, filthier and more shameless than a pig.

162. Oh . . . Life: don't threaten me with death.
Don't emphasize your hollows and shortness.
I have experienced enough of your joys and pains.
Pass joyfully, and don't give me more of your pains and grieves.

163. Anyone, who prays, does not become a sage like *Adham*[28].
The horsefly flies like honeybees, but would never produce honey.
Ignorance is only treatable by scientific knowledge.
The mullahs cannot treat ignorance; they add to it.

27: *Mullaist: Mullah-Ridden:* A person who unquestionably follows the teaching of Mullahs. Among the basic topics taught are: superstitions, guilt feelings, obsessive compulsive disorder, dead-worshipping, rigidity, fears, self-denial, morbidity, depression, regression, sexism, insecurity, intolerance toward other religions, torture, suicide-bombing, and spreading of ignorance. The Mullahs themselves do not practice what they preach. The more uninformed, misled, depressed, superstitious, insecure, guilt-ridden, and confused the Mullaist are, the more power and wealth the Mullahs gain. Regression to the time of Prophet Muhammad and following what he and his successors (Imams) have said and did are the goal of the Shiite Mullas, who have been ruling Iran since the Revolution in 1979. Since then, Iranians have been totally deprived of their Human Rights.

28: *Ibrahim Adham* (?-700): A Moslem sage/saint; a symbol of spiritual purity.

164. I will not follow the superstitious deeds and sermons.
I will not give a bean for thousands of fabricated narrations.
Oh . . . Omar Khayyam: be sure that I will never exchange your poems.
With the four volumes of *Osul al-Kafi*[29].

165. Hey . . . You Sheikh who are inflicted with scabs for years.
Why you are stupidly against music, mirth and cheers?
Even though you claim you are full of knowledge in Islam,
But in arts and sciences, you are stupid like your peers.

166. The men who are suffering from inferiority complex
And without healthy personality, they are immature.
They are afraid of their bosses like a mouse of a cat,
But they are ignorantly aggressive toward their wives like a lion.

167. Hey . . . You Iranians: don't allow the mullahs drown you in ignorance.
Don't follow them; they have no honesty and virtue.
Mullahs' job is to dupe you with fallacies and superstitions.
They have never smelled the fragrance of reality and intelligence.

168. Hey . . . My Iranian Fellowmen: if you are disappointed, what can I do?
If you have lost your freedom and human rights, what can I do?
I advised you don't follow the pagan, evil/wicked and moronic mullah.
But you did not listen to me, and fell in his bondage, what can I do?

169. Hey . . . My Iranian American Friends: don't have the sadness of nostalgia.
Don't regret the past when you were happy in Iran.
Even though you have been suffering as the results of mullah's deceits,
Be careful; please don't suffer from self-deception.

29: *Osul al-Kafi:* The title of a book in four volumes written by Muhammad-al-Kulainy (864-941 AD). It is a collection of close to 17,000 narrations from Prophet Muhammad and the Shiite's eleven Imams. Many Moslems believe that these books are second to Quran. There are also many Moslems who justifiably doubt the authenticity of these narrations.

170. Oh . . . Iran: how about what you were before, and what you are now?
Perhaps, it is not very easy for you to believe this.
The mullahs "took the royal cap off you head" (fraudulence in Farsi)
"And put the turban on your head as a hat" (fraudulence in Farsi).

171. Mullahs' slipper are more dangerous than warrior's boots.
Turbans are much more oppressive than royal crown.
The prayer carpets of those, who sold our country to the mullahs
Are, indeed, more squalid than dog's excrements.

172. Hey . . . You Mullah: neither you were born by God's will,
Nor you came into existence according to prayers or destiny.
Your father copulated with your mother.
So, you are the result of temporary marriage.

173. Oh . . . God: I am not asking you to do too many things.
I am only asking you to do me a very great favor.
Please, free all lonely birds from their cages,
And keep them healthy, happy and not alone anymore.

174. People who are in favor of modernity and novel ideas
Are mullah-stricken, even though they wear hat instead of turban.
There are many poets, professors, actors, and physicians,
Who are themselves thousand times more misled than Mullahs.

175. Those who returned our country to the Arabic-minded mullahs.
And they chose the ignoble mullahs to be in charge of our future.
At dawn, they promised us the heaven with nightingales,
But at the sunset, they gave us hell with vultures.

176. The Mullaists, who for the fall of Shah,
They supported the Fake Imam eagerly and foolishly.
Got drunk and like a psychotic with hallucination,
They saw the image of the Fake Imam on the moon.

177. From the day the Arabs prevailed over us,
The rays of our glory and esteem became dim.
Since the Arab-smitten mullah became our leader,
People from everywhere got surprised at our lack of insight.

178. People who seemingly protect Islam
And tell stories about the niceties of the Prophet,
In their fake roles as *Ayatollah*[30],
They commit a crime every moment under the name of religion.

179. Do you know why the laughter has left your lips?
And your hearts have been drowned in grief?
Your Mullaistic foolishness has reached such a high level
That it helped you to let the Akhounds to be in charge of your future.

180. The man who supported the Shah
And against the Akhounds, he did what he could.
As soon as the things changed in Akhounds' favor,
He became a mullah and began preaching.

181. Hey . . . You Doctor: although you are professionally famous,
And you revive those who are on the path of death,
If the results of physical examinations of your patient are negative,
Then, you should conclude that your patient is mentally ill.

182. The Islamic leaders, whom you consider to be an ayatollahs.
If you evaluate them intelligently, you will find out they are Pest-o-Allah.
Based on their ignorance and narrow mindedness,
You better call them Ass-o-Allah or Shit-o-Allah.

30: Ayatollah: "The Sign of God": A Moslem theologian with high status and authority, who believes in theocratic government and rigidly follows the Quran and what Muhammad and his successors had said and done. Supposedly, he represents the Absent Imam (Mahdi). As representative of God and his apostles, he can make Fatwas (Decrees) and impose them on Moslems. People who do not adhere to and follows the Decrees will be severely punished, even by execution.

183. Oh . . . My Dear Iran: have the sheikhs brought you a severe grief?
With their deceits, have they pulled you down of the progressive horse?
You were many years behind the scientific era,
And the mullahs have pushed you back hundred years more.

184. Don't ever expect absolute happiness in your life.
Like a foolish man, don't expect your life to be free of sadness.
Don't ask God for an impossible reward.
If you are not generous to others, don't expect God to be generous to you.

185. Hey . . . You who saw the face of the mullah on the moon,
Except delusion, what have you learned from him?
This old, moronic, ignorant and rigid-minded mullah
Is forcefully taking you back to the era of *Omar*[31].

186. Have you ever read the Fake Imam's Treaties,
Which explain how to clean yourself if you had enema?
With the current hygienic science, his stupid suggestions
Deserve best to be thrown in the garbage can.

187. Oh . . . My Dear Iran: since I have left your lovely soil
I feel like I am buried alive in the land of different country.
Because you have been cheated and blood-ridden by the mullahs,
I have been depressed, afflicted with anguish and shedding tears.

---

*31: **Omar ibn Khattab:*** The second caliph. During his reign, Persia was invaded by the Arabs, not for spreading Islam but for mass murderer, plundering, and destroying Persian civilization. Omar unsuccessfully attempted to gather Muhammad's divine revelations as the content of Quran. He like **Uthman** (Third Caliph) and **Ali** (Fourth Caliph) were both assassinated. The Quran was written about fifty years after Muhammad's death. It contains his revelations, which were recalled by many individuals who heard him expressing then. Fearing assassination in Mecca, Muhammad went to Medina.

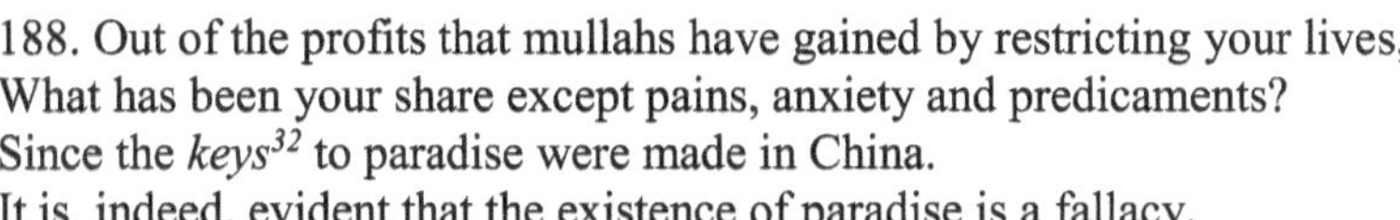

188. Out of the profits that mullahs have gained by restricting your lives,
What has been your share except pains, anxiety and predicaments?
Since the *keys*[32] to paradise were made in China.
It is, indeed, evident that the existence of paradise is a fallacy.

189. The people who claim they have created wonders,
And they also claim they have done *Imamate*[33] and made miracles.
They plunder the wealth of our country (Iran)
And put the blame on the ewer robber.

190. Oh . . . Iran: from the moment that the shah was forced to leave you,
Your conditions have drastically changed under mullahs 'dictatorship.
From the moment the Akhound's turban replaced the royal crown,
Thousand predicaments have been added to your problems.

191. Come on, and let us all be each other's good friends.
And like the seeds in a fruit become united.
Let us be a solid army with one thought, brave and homophonous.
Seeking our goals and whatever is right and good.

32: Keys: During the nine to ten years of Iran-Iraq War, Iranian soldiers were given the key to paradise. The keys were, however, ordered by the Iranian government and made in China.

33: Imamate: Functioning as an Imam guiding the Moslems in all spheres of life in the absence of the Twelve Imam. This Shiite Moslems are called the "Twelvers" because they have twelve Imam as Muhammad's successors. The Twelfth Imam (Mahdi) is expected to appear along with Jesus to save the world from bondage of blasphemy and heresy. He disappeared 1,300 years ago.

192. Hey . . . Mullah: Come on and don't riddle your gibberish.
Don't kill people, and don't commit the sin of *Ghabeel[34]*.
And with your delusional and foolish sermons,
Don't contaminate the genuine Islam for your profits.

193. Hey . . . Iranian Islamic leader: you are more brutal than *Zahaak[35]*.
You are more insane than *Hitler[36]*.
If you and shah are compared impartially,
You are thousands time worse than he was.

194. Hey . . . You Akhounds: why you are sarcastic toward Omar, the Caliph.
And you have falsely claimed to be an imam.
Your thoughts and deeds point to the fact that in your entire life,
You have been in the bondage of ignorance and delusions.

34: Gha'beel (Cain): The first child and son of Adam and Eve, who killed his younger brother, Abel. This is the first homicide, fratricide (brother-killing), sibling rivalry, family violence, and human burial in the history of monotheism. Cain learned from a crow, which was digging a hole on the ground with its beak, to dig a grave for burying the body of his brother, Abel.

35: Zahaak: A legendary tyrant king who had two living snakes on his shoulders. He fed the snakes with the brains of humans, whom he killed every day. He is the symbol of brutality and incivility.

36: Hitler, Adolph (1889-1945): Germany's tyrant leader who killed millions of Jews in Europe. In many prisons, he massed murdered the prisoners (mostly Jews) by gas. German physicians conducted fatal and unethical surgeries on the prisoners. Faced with military defeat, Hitler killed himself with a gunshot. But his wife (Eva Braun) killed herself with cyanide.

195. The Mullaist who was a perfumer during shah's reign.
He became a veterinarian right after the *Mullahs' Revolution*[37].
Without attending medical school, he now practices medicine
And dances and drinks wine before *Eftar*[38].

196. The man who was financially destitute,
And during shah's reign was a porter.
During the ruling of mullahs who nourished ignorance
Wore a white turban and became a fortuneteller.

37: *Mullahs' Revolution:* The religious revolt against Iranian kingdom led by Ruhollah Khomeini in 1979. Since 1979, the Iranian Government has been ruled by the Mullahs, who have deprived the Iranians of their Human Rights, which were first composed by Cyrus the Great, the king of Persia. Due to the pathological oppression created by the Mullahs in Iran, the rates of mental disorders, such as major depression, suicide, addiction, family violence, prostitution, sexual identity disorders, sexism, and intolerance, like physical pathologies, have drastically increased.

38: *Eftar (El Fithero):* Breaking the fast at sunset during the month of Ramadan. Fasting is one of the pillars of Islam. Prophet Muhammad received his first revelation from God in Ramadan, while he was meditating in Hira Cave. The rest of revelations were communicated three years later.

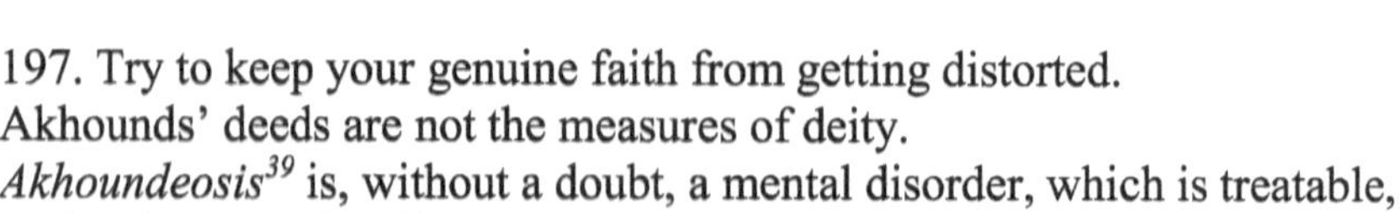

197. Try to keep your genuine faith from getting distorted.
Akhounds' deeds are not the measures of deity.
Akhoundeosis[39] is, without a doubt, a mental disorder, which is treatable,
In the absence of mullahs by mental health professionals.

198. The mullah who has sacrificed your human rights for religion,
And under the umbrella of faith he has made our country bloody.
He is so certain about your lack of wisdom and realistic orientation
That he now has keys to heaven that he ordered China to make them.

199. The scientist who wore bowtie during the reign of the Shah,
And frequently wore red and blue hats.
As soon as the Shah was forced to leave and the Mullah arrived,
He wore the turban and pretended to be like a lunatic.

39: *Akhoundeosis:* A complex mental disorder characterized with illusions, delusions, superstitions, hallucinations, and many religious and racial prejudices taught by the Akhounds. The afflicted patients experience depression, anxiety, guilt feelings, fear of God, regression, fear of death, abusive thoughts an action towards women and Non-Moslems, rigidity, obsession-compulsion, suicide, close-mindedness, dead-worshipping, beliefs in the myths of Heaven and Hell as well as in Aha'dith'(narrations) attributed to Prophet and Eleven Imams. The Twelfth Imam has disappeared but is supposed to reappear along with Jesus and Lot and other Apostles. The Akhounds have been irrational, and anti-humanitarian deeds. Basically, spreading ignorance is the major objective of most Islamic religious leaders, who all deprive their followers of Humanitarian Perspective, Religious Tolerance, Gender Equalities, and Reality Orientation.

200. Hey *Khalkhaali*[40]: You are certainly the *Shimr*[41] of this era.
And many *Jins*[42] are nesting in your body and soul.
Who was the stupid psychiatrist who discharged you,
Untreated, from mental hospital?

201. Hey . . . You the Iranian Revolutionary Leader,
When would you start keeping your promises
Of your creeds, revolution and your government?
What has Iran gained except your oppression and injustice?

202. Hey . . . You Mullah: you are more vandal than *Pharaoh*[43].
You are more bloodthirsty than *Genghis*[44] and Hitler.
Even though you grieve the killing of Imam Hussein every year,
But you are more murderous than Yazid who had Hussein murdered.

203. Hey . . . You Poets: don't write too many lyrics about romance.
Think about your country (Iran), and stop being self-centered.
With the sword of your words go and fight the tyrant mullahs.
Don't talk nonsense, and stop worshiping pain and anguish.

204. The loyal royalist who never gossiped against the Shah,
And he gained considerable wealth out of his connection with royalists.
As soon as the Arab-smitten mullah returned to Iran,
He became a Mullaist, and talked badly against the Shah.

40: Khalkhaali, Sadegh (1926-2003): A Mullah who was the revolutionary chief justice in Iran. He was appointed by Imam Khomeini. Since he sentenced more than 1,000 people to death, he was called the "Hanging Judge". Prior to his judiciary position, he was hospitalized in psychiatric ward.

41: Shimre-Zel-Joshan: The person who personally killed Imam Hussein in Kerbela, Iraq.

42: Jins: The ghostly beings, which are mostly in the service of the devil causing Junoon (psychosis). The Jin-Ridden people become Majnoon (insane) and Possessed.

43: Pharaoh: Egyptian king who did not accept monotheism and got killed by the flood, which was miraculously created by Moses when he pointed his Staff to the Red Sea to free the Jews. After escaping, however, the Jews spent forty years to reach the Promised Land.

44: Genghis Khan (1162-1227 AD): The Chinese (Mongol) leader who brutally invaded Iran.

205. Hey . . . You, the professor in the science of neurology,
Hurry up, and for saving our country, Iran,
Implant a healthy brain in the head of our leader, because
His brain is rotten, and he has chronic gall.

206. There are many flowers which are worse than cacti.
There are many trees which are fruitful contrary to the willows.
There are many visitors of Mecca, Kerbela, and *Mashhad*[45]
Who are more sinful than Shaytan (Satan in Farsi and Arabic languages).

207. Hey . . . You Akhounds: God is not a toy to play with.
Religion is not a business for making money.
If wisdom and reality-contact of people increase,
There would be no need for your fabricated and unauthentic narrations.

208. Tell me: With the exception of the wicked mullah, who is your foe?
Are you now missing the Shah in our country?
If you believe this mullah, like Shah, has robbed you of your rights,
Tell me then, what is the difference between the two?

209. Hey . . . You the professor in the science of genetics,
You look like you are terribly worried about the countless problems of Iran.
Please for the removal of idiotic genes in the brain of supreme mullah,
Think, and do something basic which will be beneficial to Iran and
Iranians.

210. Hey . . . You tyrant and shameless mullah,
In your old age, you have become more ignorant than a donkey.
Why instead of healing the prostitutes and decreasing prostitution rate
You have decided to legalize and spread it all over in Iran?

45: Mashhad: A city in Khurasaan, Iran, where the shrine of Imam Reza, the Eighth Imam is
located.

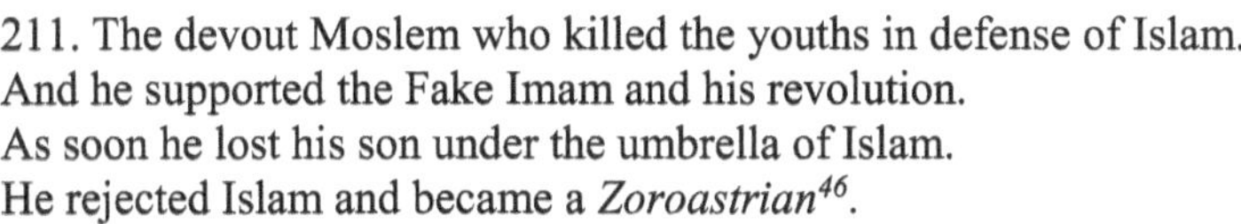

211. The devout Moslem who killed the youths in defense of Islam.
And he supported the Fake Imam and his revolution.
As soon he lost his son under the umbrella of Islam.
He rejected Islam and became a *Zoroastrian*[46].

212. Hey . . . You Supreme Leader who are the flagman of Shiism,
In intelligence, you are similar to a mule.
Don't blame the West and the East for Iran's problems, because
You are the real enemy of our country (Iran).

213. Hey . . . You the Fake Imam: you promised us a garden
And said your revolution will bring us orchards.
If, as you claim, you are a genuine patriotic Iranian leader,
Why you kill or incarcerate the patriotic Iranians?

214. Hey . . . My Friends: logic will never bow down in front of religion.
The mythological stories of mullahs do not work like medicine.
Even if the Absent *Twelfth Imam*[47] comes out of the well,
He could not solve a tiny bit of the mountain of your problems.

215. Hey . . . My Friends: I am bored with your false logic.
What have you gained from Mullaism expect anxiety disorder?
Don't blame your friends and foes for your problems.
Your lack of wisdom is the real cause of your predicaments.

46: *Zoroastrian:* Follower of Zoroastrianism, which was the religion in Persia (Iran) prior to Arab Invasion; Zaroastra was the Prophet. The pillars of Zoroastrianism are: Good Thoughts, Good Deeds, and Good Words. This religion was the first monotheism, which inspired the development of Judaism, Christianity, and Islam. Zoroastrianism has still many followers worldwide.

47: *Mahdi:* Shiiates' Twelfth Imam, who will appear to save the believers and kill the unbelievers. "The blood of the people whom he kills will cover the earth up to the knees of his horse."

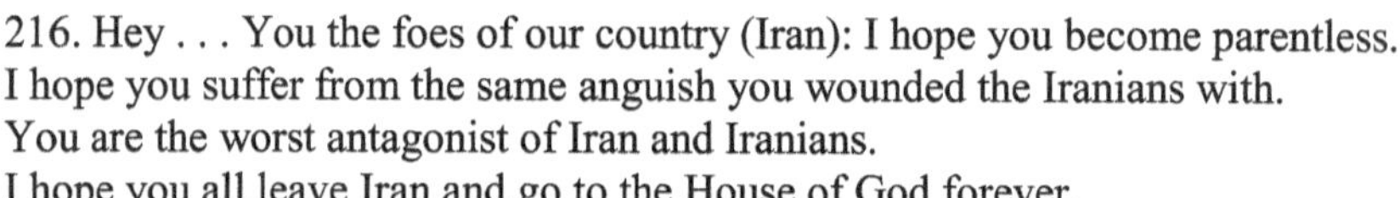

216. Hey . . . You the foes of our country (Iran): I hope you become parentless.
I hope you suffer from the same anguish you wounded the Iranians with.
You are the worst antagonist of Iran and Iranians.
I hope you all leave Iran and go to the House of God forever.

217. The man who taught the principles of *Shiism*[48] in *Qum*[49],
And he loathed debauchery, fornication and drinking wine,
With the exception of drinking wine and sleeping with harlots,
He did nothing when he came to Los Angles for a visit.

218. When the soul gets melancholic, the body feels pain.
Under the pressure of grief, the body becomes fatigued.
If we become physically ill, without the doubt, our souls,
More or less, like our bodies, gets sick and weak.

219. The mullah, who recited Quran's verses over the corpses.
And he also engraved information on tombstones in Iran.
When the brutal Supreme Leader selected him as the judge,
Out of innocent people, he ordered three death sentences per day.

220. Neither my life passed by following the misleading Akhounds,
Nor did it pass for gaining name, status or wealth.
But with the hope for the peace in the world,
I have lived fifty years under God's protection.

221. Did you see how the mullah threw the shah out of his kingdom?
And the hell he raised by robbing and killing the innocent people?
Do you know that for his own benefits, he deceitfully and debasingly
Took you out of a hole and threw you in a well?

48: *Shiism:* A sect of Islam, mostly adhered to in Iran and Iraq. It has Twelve Imams as opposed to the Sunni sect with followers who believe in Four Imams. Sunnis don't believe Imam 'Ali, Prophet's son-in-law, was a caliph. Imam 'Ali was Muhammad's cousin and became a Moslem at the age of ten.

49: *Qum:* A city south of Tehran, Iran. It has many religious schools. The shrine of Masoummah, the sister of Imam Reza (the eighth Shiite Imam) is in Qum.

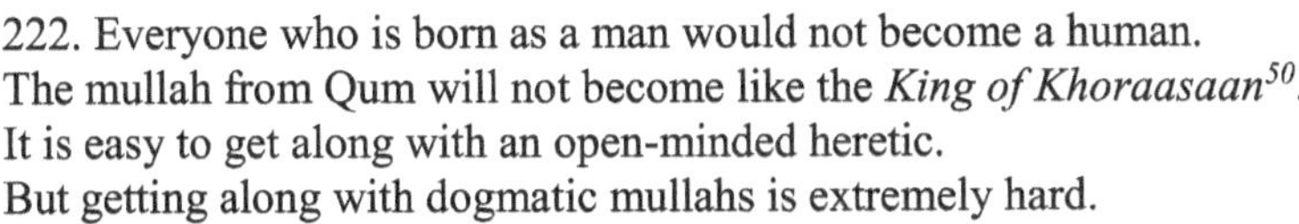

222. Everyone who is born as a man would not become a human.
The mullah from Qum will not become like the *King of Khoraasaan*[50].
It is easy to get along with an open-minded heretic.
But getting along with dogmatic mullahs is extremely hard.

223. Oh . . . God: if you help us fight and terminate mullahs' oppression
And you make equity and justice as our tradition.
The ruling of democidal mullahists,
Will be ended, benefitting our nation.

224. Oh . . . You Iranians: don't forget your glorious history.
Please remember your fame, accomplishments and worldly stature.
With science, persistence, bravery and love for our country.
Take your prudence back from your Arab-stricken enemies.

225. Hey . . . You Clergies: you are barren in creativity.
And while hallucinating, you tell us you are a sage.
For the solutions of the current world's problems,
Your old religious tools and rules have no applicability.

226. The mullahs not only benefit from your lack of knowledge,
They also block your way toward realities and truths.
I wish God will destroy the seeds of ignorance
In Iran and other Arab-ridden nations.

227. Hey . . . You Akhound: you are, indeed, the Genghis of the era.
And you have not even one sign of civility and justice.
Don't claim you have merits and scientific knowledge.
What is your collateral except your stupidity?

50: *King of Khoraasaan:* One of the titles of Imam Reza, the Eighth Shiites' Imam.

228. My Friends: the narrations of *Kuleini[51]* are all fabricated.
The rout of *Khomeini[52]* is foolish and misleading.
Seek knowledge, the truth, the reality and the genuine faith.
For how long, in Iran, you mourn for Imam Hussein's death?

229. Oh . . . God: when will we develop wisdom?
When will the era of foolishness be ended?
The mullahs say: "There is something in the hair of women.
That if men see it, they become horny."

230. Those who claim to protect Islam
And unjustifiably call themselves Imams
Interpret the Quran for gaining benefits and power.
Therefore, they commit treason against God.

231. Hey . . . You supreme power: don't lie to and deceit people.
Don't gossip against *Ferdowsi[53]* and Khayyam.
If you sacrifice yourself for Islam, we would not care at all,
But don't sacrifice our country for Islam.

232. The sheikh who wears black cloak,
And he campaigns against wine-drinking and debauchery.
He deceitfully uses religious laws to justify
His sleeping with gold diggers and drinking wine as a drug.

51: Kulaini: The author of Osoul-al-Kafi, which is a collection of Ahadith (Narrations).

52: Khomeini, Ruhollah (1902-1989): An Iranian Shiite theologian who, after years of being exiled, he, with the assistance of Iranian Mullaists and foreign powers, came back and became the leader of Islamic Republic of Iran in 1979. Since then, Iran and Iranians are ruled by theocratic, dictatorial, dogmatic, oppressive, and brutal Mullahs, who are against Human Rights and Modernity.

53: Firdowsi, Abul-Qa'sim (1904-1020 CE): An Anti-Arab Iranian epic poet, and the author of Shahnameh (The Book of Kings), which masterfully and poetically preserves the Culture and Kingdom of Iran prior to the Arabs' invasion. Shahmameh contains fifty to sixty thousand Farsi couplets.

233. My Friends: about the person who tries to deceive you,
Be careful, and don't let her/him to take advantage of you.
Run away from the person who for your pain and grieves.
Expresses more aches, anguish and worries than yourself.

234. The true believer in God does not need to follow the mullahs.
Qa'aroon[54] never asked the paupers for a penny.
If religion is forcefully imposed on people,
They would never adhere to it in their heart.

235. Oh . . . God: you know I will never separate you from my soul.
Although, I don't pray to you like others.
For whatever you have endowed me or deprived me of,
I thank you greatly and have no grievance.

236. Oh . . . My Dear Mother: if you are ill, I will sacrifice my soul for your health.
I am terribly worried about you, and praying for you.
I hope God will make you healthy and happy, otherwise,
I hope your pains and anguish will strike my heart.

237. Hey . . . You Mullah: don't make your records more squalid.
You have polluted your cloak with the blood of thousands of innocents.
You killed hundreds, who were more innocent than *Akbar and Asghar*[55].
And you justify your killing by your self-benefiting religious trivialities.

238. Hey . . . You Iranians: wake up and develop positive insight.
Avoid doubts, weakness and negligence.
And for warding off the current violence, ignorance and debasement,
Saddle your *Rakhsh*[56], sharpen your swords and decisions.

54: *Gharoon: Croesus (595-547 BC):* The king of Lydia with wealth beyond counts. Due to his disobedience of God's rules, he and his innumerable treasures were swallowed by earth.

55: *Akbar and Asghar:* Male children of Iman Hussein, who were killed in Kerbala by Yazed's troops.

56: *Rakhsh:* The name of Rustam's horse. In Ferdowsi's Shahnameh, Rustam was a Persian who was loyal, strong, and a genuine nationalist.

239. My heart is full of anguish and mourning pains.
Of the death of my mother, it has lost its peace.
For every sorrow, you can find a relief.
But the grief of becoming motherless has no recovery.

240. Oh . . . God: even though you turned off the life-light of my mother,
But don't turn off her bright light which shines in my heart.
While I am still alive, please give me an opportunity,
So I can wash her grave with my tears.

241. Tonight, I am ill because I am motherless.
I am feverish and suffering grief because she passed away.
While nostalgic, tearful, lonely and depressed tonight,
I am awake and mourning for my mother.

242. For a decade and half, we played the childish games.
During our youth, we drank wine while proud of our strength and looks.
Then afraid of the false hell, we deprived ourselves of gratifications.
And then, we died and flew to the mythical paradise.

243. Oh . . . God: help me, and debase my non-appreciative foe.
I treated him well, but he did me wrong, so please punish him.
And as long as he lives, give him pain, disasters and grief.
And make him suffer; let him be mournful every year.

244. If you doubt the purity of the water you want to use,
Listen to Imam Khomeini who gives us a beneficial advice:
"If a dog defecates on your beard, don't worry, because
The filth will be cleansed by the ray of the sun."

245. Hey . . . You incompetent, unwise and heretic Islamic Leader,
You have made our nation weak and disturbed with your ignorance.
Don't justify your insanity, thirst for blood and sexist attitude
In the name of God and according to fabricated narrations.

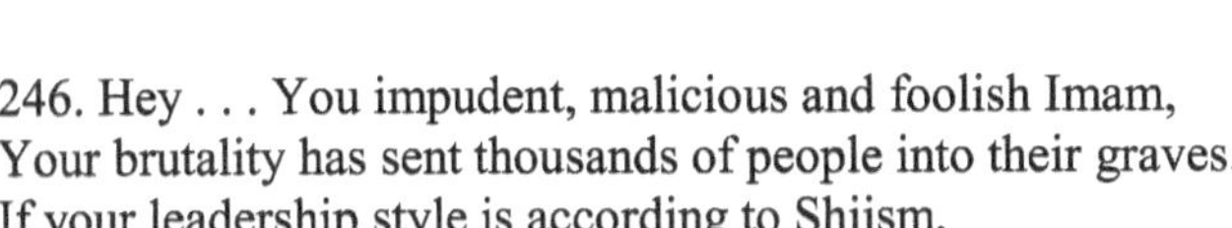

246. Hey . . . You impudent, malicious and foolish Imam,
Your brutality has sent thousands of people into their graves.
If your leadership style is according to Shiism,
Blessed be Yazid, Shimr and Zah'ak.

247. My Friends: the beginning and the end of our lives are both here.
The pains and sadness, like happiness and pleasures are all here.
Don't bribe the mullah for getting you into heaven, because
The Garden of Eden and the well of the hell are both here.

248. Hey . . . You, who complain of the pains in your back and shoulders
And moan of the sorrows of poverty and difficult time,
You are not disabled; don't pretend to be sick.
Go and get a job close to your home.

249. Hey . . . Dear Iranians: if you have zeal and ambition
And you are respectful toward your country and yourselves,
Then free your country and yourself from Akhounds' bondage.
With your nationalistic bravery, moral heroism and love for your country.

250. Hey . . . You who have robbed our country's wealth: I would not help you.
I would not teach you how to get rid of your depression and stress.
If death angel takes you to the depth of hell,
I would not be saddened, and would not pray for you.

251. My Dear Iranians: how long do you want to be enslaved?
How long for the Akhounds, you will provide free services?
With all of your oil resources, your lives are full of difficulties.
Without the oil, how would you live free of life's problems?

252. If your wealth has reached the wealth of Qa'aroon's (Croesus)
And the length of your lawn is as long as *Karoon River*[57]?
What are all these worth, if you don't help your mankind?
Let us assume that you have also gained the fame of *Aaron*[58].

---

*57: **Karoon River:*** A long river in Southern Iran.

*58: **Aaron:*** Brother and successor of Prophet Moses.

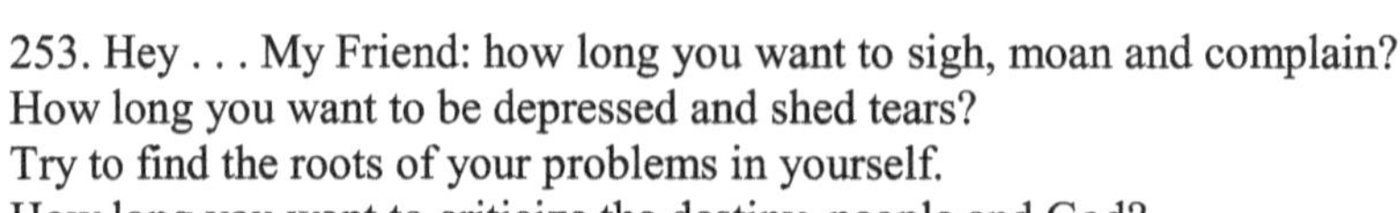

253. Hey . . . My Friend: how long you want to sigh, moan and complain?
How long you want to be depressed and shed tears?
Try to find the roots of your problems in yourself.
How long you want to criticize the destiny, people and God?

254. Do you know how fast life passes by?
And how it passes through the zigzag, ups and downs with stress?
Half of it passes with sorrows while one third passes with mirth.
And alas: one third of it has to passes through sleep.

255. General X who, for the protection of our country (Iran),
He sworn to God he will sacrifice his life for the freedom of our country.
He sold our country to a gang of dictatorial Arab-minded Akhounds.
Thus, he made his name, honor and self-esteem filthy in our history.

256. The gullible people who invested their hopes in Iranian Islamic revolution,
And they lost their sons and daughters as *Shahid*[59] during its rise.
From the dictatorial, revolutionary and oppressive government,
They gained only violence, corruption, regression, and mental illness.

257. Hey . . . You Akhound: you have intellectual decrement.
When, for the benefits of our country (Iran) you will pass away?
With the exception of brutality, poverty, corruption and national disgrace,
What else have you brought for our country and countrymen?

258. Hey . . . You Mullahs: don't broadcast the false news.
Don't keep insisting that your falsehood is correct.
Please, with absurd and unauthentic Islamic narrations,
Don't defame the Prophet and his descendants.

59: *Shahid (Martyr):* Whoever dies, gets killed, or commits suicide in the cause of God and in defending Islam. Imam Hussein is the best example. Shohadaa (the plural for Shahid) are divinely destined to go to Heaven, benefiting the full services from the Virgin Houries (girls) and Ghelmaans (boys).

259. Please, don't listen to the palmist nor believe in horoscopy.
The willow trees will never bear blossom or fruits.
Don't base your future on the dreams you have while asleep,
Such dreams are related to your past, and never predict your future.

260. Don't ever give your friend anything except help and happiness.
And share the load of your friend's anguish willingly.
Honesty and respect are the measure of friendship.
Don't ever sell wet woods to your friends[60].

261. The man who ran away from the odor of wine,
And in the eyes of others, he was purer than angels.
After he was condemned for incestuous crime,
He committed suicide while in prison.

262. Oh . . . Iranians: don't be deceived by another turban-wearing mullah.
Instead of the narrations choose another behavioral guideline.
Oh . . . God: Send us Babak *Khorramdin[61]* back soon.
So he will eliminate the *Caliphate[62]* in Iran one more time.

263. There are many judges who are more evil than the convicts.
There are many wine drinkers who are wiser than the alert sheriffs.
There are many non-Moslems, who are more humanitarian,
And they are also more faithful, wise and open-minded than ayatollahs.

264. Everyone who is wealthy, well-dressed and good-looking
May not be, as you think, free of psychological symptoms.
Wealth and appearance are not the criteria for mental health.
Mental patients have no horns or tails, my friends.

60: An Iranian Proverb: Don't ever deceive or cheat your friends.

61: Babak Khorramdin (795 AD): A Persian Zoroastrian nationalist who freed Persia from Arabic Abbasid Caliphate with the help of Maziyar, who was also a Zoroastrian nationalist.

62: Caliphate: The ruling of a Caliph who rigidly follows Islamic Laws and Narrations.

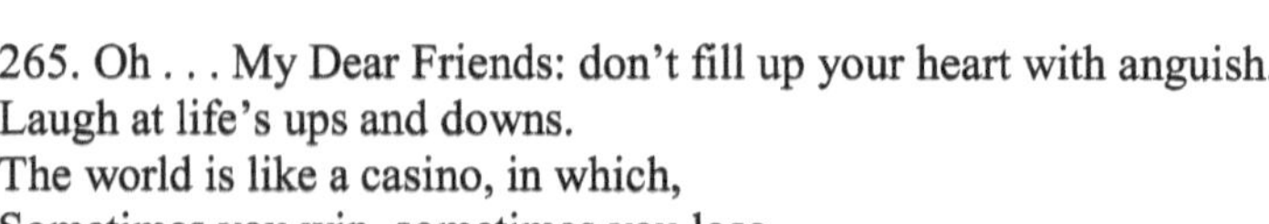

265. Oh . . . My Dear Friends: don't fill up your heart with anguish.
Laugh at life's ups and downs.
The world is like a casino, in which,
Sometimes you win, sometimes you lose.

266. The Mullah who writes falsified narrations,
And he denies he has two concubines.
When his sister became the concubine of another mullah,
Of shame, he divorced his concubines and condemned prostitution.

267. Hey . . . Mullah: don't boast about your decency.
Your sermons do not match the truth and reality.
Except spreading whoredom, falsehood, brutality and terror,
What have been the real gifts of your bloody revolution?

268. Hey . . . You who are poisoned by absurdities, dogmatism and superstitions,
Do you know why you are condemned to slavery?
As long as the Akhounds rule you and your country,
You will be deprived of all of your human rights.

269. Oh . . . Poets: how long you moan of the unkindness of your beloved?
How long you describe her beautiful figure, eyes and mole?
About the pains our countrymen has, however,
How long and why you are so insensitive and negligent?

270. The people who sound nice like nightingale,
If you look at them deeply, they are really bats.
Be aware that most Akhounds, Rabbi, preachers and priests.
Are all of the same essence in deceitfulness and charlatanism.

271. While the lives of many pass through without dispute or haggle,
Many lives pass with sadness, pains and adversities.
Alas, the unfortunate are those who under the yoke of dictators.
Their lives pass fast and regressively, but never progressively.

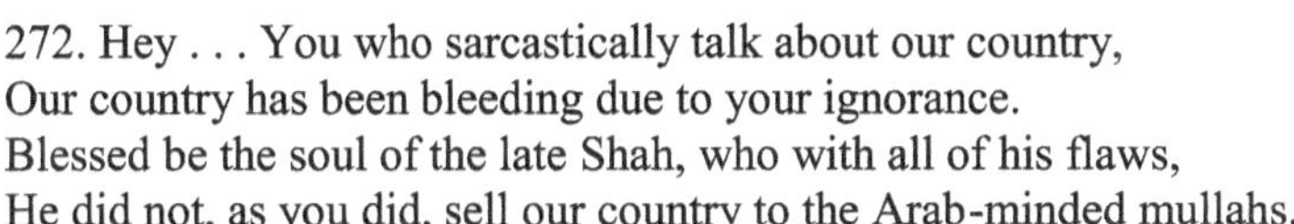

272. Hey . . . You who sarcastically talk about our country,
Our country has been bleeding due to your ignorance.
Blessed be the soul of the late Shah, who with all of his flaws,
He did not, as you did, sell our country to the Arab-minded mullahs.

273. Hey . . . You, who beat your chest for the love of our country,
Why did you, like the mullahs, fight against our nation?
If you support the Akhounds' government,
You are, like them, the cause of the disasters in our country.

274. Hey . . . Akhound: don't try to impose the narrations on me.
Don't distort the true faith for your benefits and power.
Throw the books of narrations in a well.
And don't distort true religion with your absurd sermons.

275. Oh . . . My Friends: the orbit and you are in debt to me.
Because: My job is treating the mentally disturbed patients.
If your wealth includes many castles, jewels and treasures of gold.
My wealth is the health and happiness of my patients.

276. If, as you claim: You are now healthy and intelligent?
And tell me you are honest and law-abiding,
Then why do you want me, contrary to your health,
To write a report indicating that you are mentally ill?

277. My Dear Friends: don't support the vulgar Akhounds.
Don't help the wicked and procuress mullahs.
These people lack scientific and artistic aptitudes.
Never expect to get milk out of a baby goat.

278. Hey . . . Sheikhs: it is none of your business if I am not a hajji.
I will never pay you a bribe for anything.
In dealing with God and Satan,
I do not need a mediator or middleman like you.

279. Don't listen to those who are sweet talkers,
Nor be deceived by those who are well-behaved.
The savagery of the two-footed beast, named Human.
Is, sometimes, worse than hyena's wildness.

280. Although the mullahs have stored hilarity in their own hearts,
They have planted the seeds of misery in yours.
During the past fourteen centuries, under the name of religion,
The mullahs have kept you far away from having contact with reality.

281. Hey . . . Mullahs: the road of life is much smoother without you.
The tree of science is more fruitful in your absence.
My blasphemous neighbor is hundred times more humanistic
Than the Supreme Leader, who leads you in prayer at the mosques.

282. Hey . . . You Girl who owe everything you own to your beauties,
You are so narcissistic that you hate the moon (symbol of beauty in Farsi).
Based on the science of genetics, are you aware
That you and chimpanzees are genetically close to ninety percent alike?

283. Oh . . . Dear Lady: you are as beautiful as an angel.
Have you ever asked yourself about your evolution?
During many millions of years,
You evolved from a single-celled organism to a human.

284. If you are happy or sad about the universe,
And if you are proud of yourself or have low self-esteem,
No matter what you are, God is not responsible.
You are the product of heredity and environment.

285. Hey . . . My Countrymen: wake up and leave the state of laziness.
If you have self-worth and capability, you have the option of
Either uprooting the cacti of ignorance,
Or regress back to the era of Arab paganism.

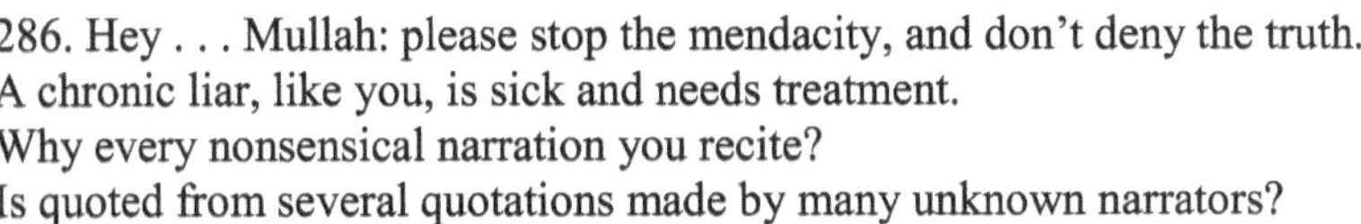

286. Hey . . . Mullah: please stop the mendacity, and don't deny the truth.
A chronic liar, like you, is sick and needs treatment.
Why every nonsensical narration you recite?
Is quoted from several quotations made by many unknown narrators?

287. One day I with my wealth, youth and looks,
Took a trip along with insight, life and death.
First, my life robbed me of my looks, wealth and youth.
And then, death opened its wings toward my life.

288. Oh . . . Dear Iranians: how long should you be the slaves of the idiots?
Why you are like toys in the hands of the vile?
In gaining your human rights, respect and freedom,
Why don't you use your bravery, strength, love for Iran and solidarity?

289. Austerity and hypocrisy don't make the mullahs the men of God.
A tavern will not become a mosque with reciting the holy revelations.
Take the cotton of ignorance out of your ears and listen well.
The lead never turns into gold by prayers.

290. Oh . . . Iran: what authority or power do you have now?
Among the nations, what credence do you own?
As long as you are under the rules of Akhounds,
What do you expect to have, except weakness and vulnerabilities?

291. Hey . . . you incompetent ayatollah who are misled and boastful,
And in benefitting the country, you are full of deceits.
There is no trace of deity and civility in you.
You are Iran's enemy, and deserve to be called Ayatoll-Satan.

292. If you have not read the poetry of Khayyam
And have not tasted the wine of his realistic advices,
How can you carry the load of your sorrows
Without the power of love and the warmth of wine?

293. Hey . . . Doctor: although your speech is very informative.
But every living thing is finally doomed to die.
But, please don't lose your hope in treating the women,
Who have the symptoms of breast cancer.

294. My Dear Wife: I will not trade one of your eyelashes for tons of women's hair.
I will not trade one single hair of yours with hundred angels.
I will not trade one of your meaningful and beautiful frowns
With the smiles of hundred women who have pretty eyes.

295. The one who had not tamed his animalistic soul
And claimed he has not committed even a sin
Following the advice of Imam Khumeini, and with the consent of his wife,
He married the under-aged daughter of his sister-in-law.

296. Hey . . . You President Mullah: your sermons lack total applicability.
Why your thoughts and your leader's thoughts are not matched?
The leader has given you only the handle of the knife.
But the knife without the blade has no cutting power.

297. Oh . . . My dear friends: if you have a bodily illness
And your soul is full of anguish and affliction,
Be aware that every reaction you experience within you
Is the manifestation of the roles and functions of your brain.

298. There is a sheikh whose tongue is like the stinging tail of a scorpion
And is a professor of superstitions in city of Qum.
Hey you Mullah: give him my message.
I have been against superstition and delusions since my childhood.

299. Without love and wisdom, life is a mirage.
Without wine and music, the soul is bored.
If you compare the length of your life with that of the universe,
Your life is hundred times shorter than the life of a bubble.

300. Hey . . . Mullahs: what I am saying is neither for fighting you,
Nor it is a heresy or against piety.
To discriminate against women is incorrect and insulting
Even though, it might be a Quran's verse, or an Imam's decree.

301. My dear wife Lili: Be sure that loving you is my creed.
When you are away, my heart hurts me.
From the moment you have left this town,
Sadness has been my friend, and tears have been my sympathizer.

302. Hey . . . Mullah: is something disturbing your mind?
Why do you interfere with the works of poets?
Go and dust off your pulpit of your deceitfulness
With the cloth you have on your head as a turban.

303. Hey . . . You Akhound who always appear praising the God
And assert that except obeying God you have no job or hobby.
If your belief in God is as genuine as you claim,
Why do you behead the people with your prejudicial ax?

304. Hey . . . You Arab-smitten Mullah: don't kill the patriotic sages.
Discharge the freedom-seekers from your hellish prisons.
With your brutality, oppression, ignorance and threats,
Don't sadden those whom you have already afflicted.

305. Hey . . . You, who have come with the hope for an eternal life.
Alas, that you have come to be doomed to nonexistence.
While alive, however, be happy and don't ask fruitlessly,
By whose will, wherefrom, and why you came to this world?

306. The beauty of full moon reminds me of your color and face.
It also makes me think of your sad and myth-telling eyes.
The ups and downs in the waves of ocean
Remind me of your body and temper.

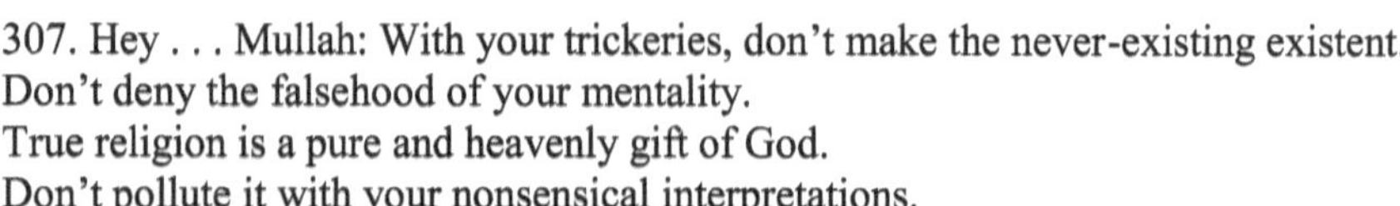

307. Hey . . . Mullah: With your trickeries, don't make the never-existing existent.
Don't deny the falsehood of your mentality.
True religion is a pure and heavenly gift of God.
Don't pollute it with your nonsensical interpretations.

308. Those who, revolted against the Shah
And foolishly, gave the title of imam to a mullah,
They now worship mullah's grave as an idol,
Exactly, like the pagan Arabs prior to the rise of Islam.

309. Hey You who have become spelled by the mullahs' bewitchment
And you have become involved in the bloody revolution,
If you open your eyes and impartially analyze your circumstances,
You will realize that you have been cheated by the revolution.

310. Come on and let us dance on one of these nights
And logically discuss the essence of life and love.
Let us learn about the art of intimacy
And then review them with kisses and a cup of wine.

311. Oh . . . Dear Ladies: be alert and don't let the Akhounds abuse you.
And don't let them afflict you with their stupidity and sexist attitudes.
I swear to God that, contrary to what the abusive mullah's claim,
Writing prayers on your love handle will never make you pregnant.

312. Hey you Arab-ridden mullahs who are far away from wisdom.
Don't change the locations of the people's grave sites for your profit.
The day will come when the new generation, for the benefit of our country,
Will eagerly and repeatedly, transfer your corpse from one grave to another.

313. With the exception of mullahs' poisoned-food, what have you been eating?
What benefit are you trying to seek from his rotten grave?
When they exhume the graves of few Akhounds,
There was nothing found except the remains of mules.

314. Oh . . . Dear Iran: we should sacrifice our souls for you.
We should pay our debts to you with appreciation
If you want to regain your freedom and be progressive,
You should separate religion from government.

315. Hey . . . My Friends: illness is not treatable with oblations.
The pistachio will never smile with incantation.
You can achieve your goals only with wisdom and action.
The scientist cannot conquer the galaxies with prayers and donation.

316. Hey . . . Mullahs: Now you have become more heretic and unrealistic.
You have become infatuated by the deed of Lucifer.
Don't murder the youths in the name of religion.
You are, indeed, more blood-thirsty than Attila the *Hun*[63].

317. The sheikh who is defending the principles of Islam
And as a *Sayyid*[64] and dervish, he recites the Holy Verses.
He got married only to save face, because
In spite of wearing such a bushy and long beard, he is *Beardless*[65].

318. *Khatami*[66]: I am asking you without any fears.
What happened to the promises and many vows you made?
If you don't keep your promises, and break your vows,
Then, your promises are as worthless as a bean.

319. The wealthy ones who wear golden attires,
They will finally be buried in their grave-clothes.
This world is just like a hotel that from its two doors.
One hundred thousand people arrive and exit per day.

63: ***Attila the Hun:*** The brutal ruler of Hunnic (Eastern Europe) Empire during AD 433-453.

64: ***Sayyid:*** A Moslem who is, by birth, a relative of the descendant of Prophet Mohammad.

65: ***Beardless (Bereesh):*** In Farsi (Iranian) language, it means homosexual.

66: ***Khatami, Mohammad:*** A Mullah who was the president of Iran (1997-2005).

320. From the fire of true love, I am full of sparkles.
In the autumn of life, I feel like spring.
Although I look much younger than my age,
Don't give me an evil eye; I am sixty-four now.

321. Those who only think of and take care of themselves,
And like the thin-bearded men, they are wishing for bushy beard.
They will never do any good to others, because
They seem to belong to the generation of buffalo.

322. The Mullaist who has become the Iranian minister of guidance
Asserted: "The country will become pure and flourishing in ethics."
However, prostitution via temporary marriage has become the fad.
And the use of opium and alcohol has become secretly more frequent.

323. Hey . . . My Friends: do you know why you have become crazy lately,
And why you have become negligent in protecting our country?
Because due to your disease of Akhoundeosis.
You have become misled and drowned in insipidity.

324. Hey . . . Young Iranian Generation: you are worthy of success.
Mullahs' goals are to keep you weak and superstitious forever.
Obtain your freedom from these dogmatic creatures, because
Your freedom is the guarantee for your glorious future.

325. Hey . . . You, the Ayat-ul-Satan: do you know?
In terms of shame and honor, you are behind animals?
Finally one day, people will take the mask off your face
And will realize that you are unscrupulous, sordid, wicked.

326. Hey . . . Iranians: Why don't you use your bravery and capability?
Go and find the bread, why you are worried about the water?
In the era when the sciences and technology are blossoming,
Why fruitlessly, you are expecting miracles?

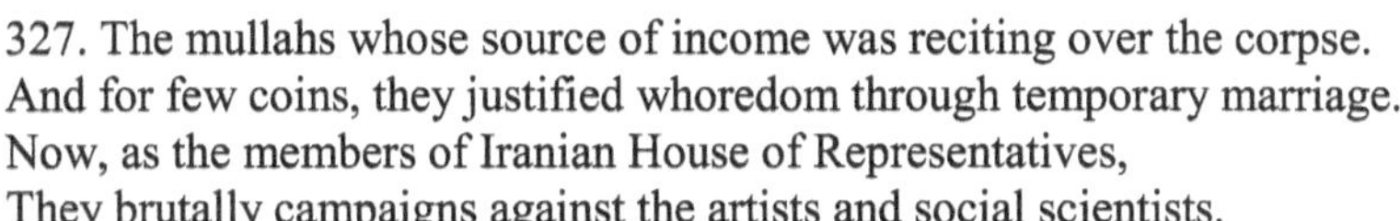

327. The mullahs whose source of income was reciting over the corpse.
And for few coins, they justified whoredom through temporary marriage.
Now, as the members of Iranian House of Representatives,
They brutally campaigns against the artists and social scientists.

328. Hey . . . Iranians: What happened to your *Sassanid*[67] power
And the courage and patriotism you learned from *Mazdak*[68] and *Mani*[69]?
Whoever deprives you of your freedom
Will also tramples on all of your human rights.

329. The mullah who left for Mecca, but due to his illness, he arrived in Turkestan.
And his murderous deeds have drastically expanded the graveyards in Iran.
From his thoughts, behavior and speech, it is clear that
He has been discharged from mental institution untreated.

330. My dear Lili: since you took your trip, I have missed you terribly.
I hear your voice every single moment and see you in my dreams.
Even though, I spend some of my time with our friends,
But my heart keeps flapping for you, my dearest.

331. The person who complained of poverty and sorrows
And talked about his appreciation for what other did for him,
After his predicaments were resolved with my assistance,
He started gossiping against me.

332. If your patient sighs and moans of aches
And of pain and discomfort, his body has stooped.
Even though his symptoms appear to be all physical,
But his illness has, without a doubt, a psychological dimension.

67: Sassanid: Persian kingdom at the time of Arab invasion.

68: Mazdak (?-528 BC): A Persian moralist/socialist who claimed to be God's prophet/apostle.

69: Mani (216-274 AD): A Persian Gnostic, who claimed to be God's prophet/apostle. He was the founder of Mannichaeism as a sect of Zoroastrianism.

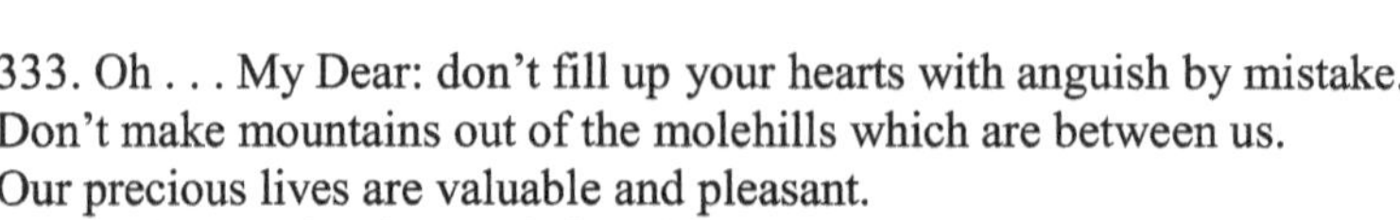

333. Oh . . . My Dear: don't fill up your hearts with anguish by mistake.
Don't make mountains out of the molehills which are between us.
Our precious lives are valuable and pleasant.
Please don't make them painful with your verbal stings.

334. Hey . . . Mullahs: Why don't you try to seek the truth and reality?
When will you be free of ignorance and idiotic daydreaming?
Human being has a dynamic nature, while your doctrine is static.
The static will never be useful for the dynamic.

335. When will the seeds of wisdom be planted in human brains?
When with the crop of wisdom, the fabric of science and art will be weaved?
Alas, the artistic and scientific potentials of millions of Iranians are,
Like their love for their country, oppressed under the name of religion.

336. Hey . . . You Mullaist: you are, indeed, misled and mentally disturbed.
The scientific rout is opposite the path your Arab-minded leader suggests.
Go and visit a mental health professional as soon as possible.
So you will find out the causes of your disturbance and the right trail of life.

337. If you moan of the pains of kidney stone,
Eat watermelon every night.
If your glaucoma is getting worse,
Use prescribed marijuana or hempseed.

338. Even though your coins of gold are more than the desert sands
And your kitchenwares are made out of silver and gold,
But if you don't help your needy humankind,
You will be better off to live with animals.

339. Hey . . . Akhounds: you are full of flaws in reality and wisdom.
Where God has discussed the hairs of women as sexual stimulant?
If women's hair and your animalistic sexuality are stupidly associated,
The women are innocent; you are the one who is weak and horny.

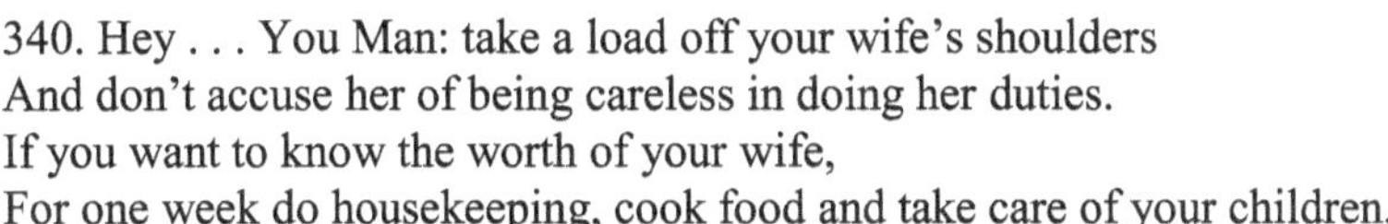

340. Hey . . . You Man: take a load off your wife's shoulders
And don't accuse her of being careless in doing her duties.
If you want to know the worth of your wife,
For one week do housekeeping, cook food and take care of your children.

341. If you are complaining of your husband's temperament
Ask yourself what triggers his distress and anger.
Search in yourself and find out which of your traits
Provoke your husband's vulnerable reactions?

342. Before you become forever incarcerated in the ground,
You better free yourself from the prison of ignorance.
In search for reality, how long you want to be,
Lost in delusions and superstitions?

343. The sheikh who claims to be a religious jurisprudent,
And he is impudent in his thoughts, deeds and sermons.
In the sciences of governing and peacekeeping, however,
He is also impotent and intolerant, my friends.

344. Go on and pick up a flower, although it has thorns.
Go on and find a treasure, although it may have a snake.
Go on and frequently visit your dear friends,
Even though, they have angry and untamed dogs.

345. Hey . . . Mullahs: except the agony, what women have gained from you?
Their prime problems are your discrimination and prejudice against them.
If the hair of women awaken your animalistic sexuality,
Your bushy and harsh beards hurt their skin and kill their passion.

346. Oh . . . God: I have a firing anguish in my heart.
Because: my dear friend is ill.
Oh . . . God: please do me a great favor,
Make him to recover and keep him healthy.

347. Hey . . . My Friends: avoid mullahs' worthless sermons.
Defeat his ignorance with the aid of scientific intelligence.
Your faith in superstitions, narrations and fate
Flourishes mullahs' profession, and increases his income and power.

348. Tonight, I am without pains and sorrows.
I am full of compassion and desires for world's peace.
Spiritually, I feel like I am five thousand years old
While morphologically, I am only sixty-five.

349. Hey . . . Mullahs: have you been eating the brains of donkeys?
For how long like snakes, you sting the artists and realists?
I hope the day will come when the artists and scientists
Will take revenge for your animosity toward arts and sciences.

350. Hey . . . You Girl: who are so proud of your youth and beauty,
Don't make fun of and ridicule the elderly.
One day the elderly were young and beautiful like you,
And one day you too will become aged and unattractive like them.

351. Listen to me friends: pledging your mind to the mullahs is wrong.
And carrying their loads, like a mule, by force is an error.
To become a martyr for the love of our country is justified,
But martyrdom for spreading ignorance and terrorism is incorrect.

352. Hey . . . You Lady: who possess beauty, charm and charisma,
Be aware: you are the source of intelligence and diversity.
Don't give the mullahs the opportunity to, for their benefits,
Steal your right and block your path toward developing your potentials.

353. Hey . . . You: who complain of your pains and problems,
Why you are so far away from realizing the reality?
If you want to earn back your human rights from the mullahs,
You better first gain your self-worth and merits.

354. Hey . . . Mullah: although your voice sounds nice,
But the content of your sermon is absurd and ridiculous.
Any religion which blocks the progress of human mind and spirit is
Incapable of inspiring human to go through the sociocultural evolution.

355. Hey . . . You Akhounds: why you are planning for pilgrimage to Mecca?
You all have thousands of deceits under your turbans.
Don't be disrespectful toward God by going to Mecca, because
You all have thousands of drops of the blood of innocents on your cloaks.

356. Oh . . . Iran: earn back your might, power and dignity.
Get your jurisdiction and human rights back from the mullahs.
As long as you are afflicted with the symptoms of Akhoundeosis, however,
You will never find your credibility, honor and self-respect.

357. Before the dust embraces you forever.
Don't try any routes except the path of true love and science.
If you want to be free from mullahs' absurdities
Put the cotton of wisdom in your ears.

358. Hey . . . You: the victims of mullahs' collusions and secret deals,
Your mentality is, without a doubt, the source of his existence and power.
You are afflicted with Akhoundeosis, because due to your lack of insight.
You have allowed the mullahs to control your thoughts and deeds.

359. What benefits do you earn from criticism and denial of modernity?
What do you gain from augury, oblation, and reciting the Holy Verses?
Free yourself from superstitions and absentmindedness
And go after science, arts, water/food and true love.

360. Whoever allows the Akhounds to control her/his life
Would never benefits from the fruits of sciences and arts.
There are many blossoms of talents in science and art which
Die under the oppressive pressure of the mullahs.

361. Hey . . . Mullahs: you are rotten in essence.
Why you seek for reality in the mirage?
The truth is time and place bound.
Don't talk nonsense; how long you are going to be asleep?

362. The Akhounds never honestly narrate the truth.
Watch out: their ignorance is, indeed, contagious.
With the exception of science and contact with reality,
Nothing else will lead you toward God.

363. Hey . . . You Mullaists: take a good look at yourself
And then try to find a cure for your distorted cognition.
While you follow the unauthentic narrations,
The non-Moslems send satellites to the galaxies.

364. Hey . . . Iranian Mullahs: you are superstitious and worship the intangibles.
Your free-loading lifestyle began with the appearance of Islam.
A day will come when man with the help of God,
Will get rid of you; you are mean, deceitful, barbarian and our enemy.

365. Mullah: azan (calling for prayer) does not help scientific endeavors.
Your sermons, verse reciting and assumptions don't contain wisdom.
Go to mosque and give sermons there, because
The university is not a mosque.

366. My Iranian Friends: who has made you debased and frail?
Do you know why your lives have been so tied up?
The mullahs have, in the name of religion, robbed
Your freedom to think, behave and speak.

367. My dear Countrymen: get realistic and don't be a dervish any more.
Don't follow the Akhounds; follow a genuine faith.
In your attempts to free our country from the darkness of ignorance,
Seek for the solutions with a scientific torch.

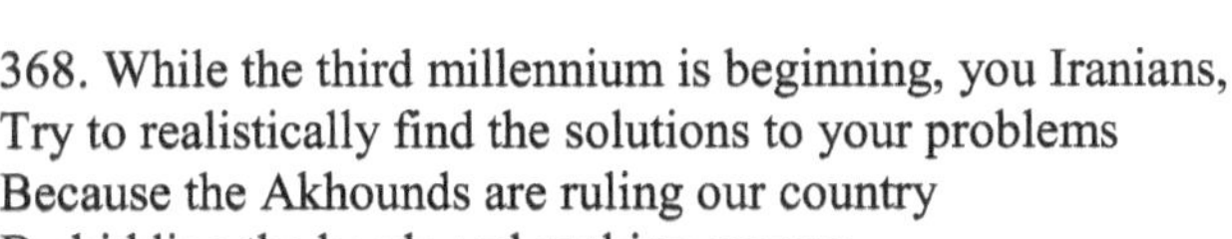

368. While the third millennium is beginning, you Iranians,
Try to realistically find the solutions to your problems
Because the Akhounds are ruling our country
By bidding the beads and seeking augury.

369. Prayers don't make the country run well like in era of Jam (Persian king).
The sheikhs cannot defend the country like Rustam (Persian hero).
The country will flourish with science and action,
Not by religion, from which no science can be derived.

370. Do you know why you have become frail and flimsy?
And you have been deprived of the eagerness and happiness of living?
Because: the Akhounds, for their own profits, have associated fears with insecurities,
depression, guilt, anguish and morbidity in your mind.

371. Hey . . . You Blasphemous Mullahs: God is not for sale.
Deceits, tricks and robe-wearing are not criteria for genuine spirituality.
Don't steal the wealth of our nation in the names of God and religion.
Stealing is never the signs of intelligence.

372. Hey . . . You, who complain of the Akhounds
And of their injustice, you have two hundred grievances.
Don't grumble; but with your wisdom, hopes and endeavors
Earn your rights if you have efficiency and worthiness.

373. Except tribulation, what have you received from the Akhounds?
They have degraded your high status and worth.
If you don't gain back your human rights and freedom from them,
Then you are worthy of them as they are worthy of you.

374. Do you know why you are idle and shortsighted?
And instead of using your wisdom, you make recital and oblation?
Because during the past fourteen centuries your brain has been
Addicted to Mullaism, which has blocked your path to creative thinking.

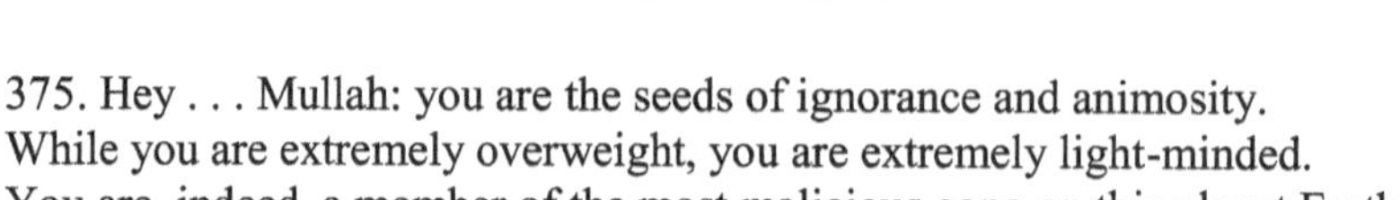

375. Hey . . . Mullah: you are the seeds of ignorance and animosity.
While you are extremely overweight, you are extremely light-minded.
You are, indeed, a member of the most malicious gang on this planet Earth.
In fact, you are worse than the murderer in *Finn's Bath*[70].

376. Hey... Mullahs: tell me, except the cloak you wear what is your load?
With the exception of human blood, with what food you break your fast?
And aside from satisfying your animalistic needs and fool-making,
What are your ideology, objectives, and job in life?

377. Hey . . . Iranians: don't suffer any more for your life's problems.
Cleanse your soul of the superstitions, dogmatism and narrow-mindedness.
Seek for the real determinants of the ups and downs in your life.
Logical reasoning negates religious delusions and negative fantasies.

378. Hey . . . You Mullah: don't think you are highly respectful.
And don't claim you were born to reputable and legally-married parents.
I heard from your uncle, the *Friday Imam*[71] of the city
That you, like your sister, were born illegitimately.

379. We should call God now through our genuine prayers
And request him to ward off our current calamities.
Religion has become a toy in the hands of mullahs.
Therefore, it must be freed from their influence now.

380. My friends: don't fruitlessly moan about life's challenges.
You yourself might have a role in causing your sorrows.
You will never experience the pleasure in your life
As long as you worship religious delusions and hallucinations.

70: *Finn's Bath:* A public bath in Finn, Kashan, Iran where Mirza Taghi Khan Amir Kabir (1807-1852), who was the Prime Minister of Nasser al-Din Qajar (Iranian King), was murdered. Amir Kabir was a reformist and modernizer who made many contributions to the advancement of Persian society. He was a Moslem, and in spite of his nationalistic devotion, he ordered the murdering of many Bahais, the followers of Bab, the founder of Bahaism. He also ordered the murder of Bab (1850) in Tabriz, Iran.

71: *Friday Imam:* The Chief Mullah in charge of religious activities in a city.

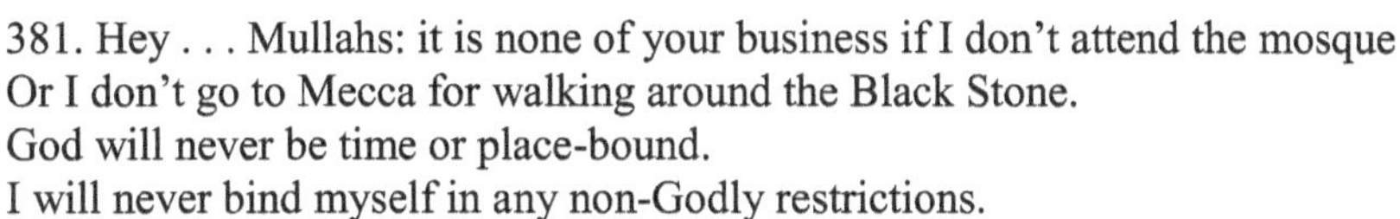

381. Hey . . . Mullahs: it is none of your business if I don't attend the mosque
Or I don't go to Mecca for walking around the Black Stone.
God will never be time or place-bound.
I will never bind myself in any non-Godly restrictions.

382. Oh . . . God: in thanking you for Lili (my wife), I don't have enough words.
Lili is the soul of my body and the ointment for my pains.
If you wish, separate all the joints in my body from one another,
But please don't separate her from me.

383. Although my life has passed through many ups and downs,
But it is now passing through happily, successfully and lightly.
While helping my fellowmen, inquiring knowledge and loving Iran,
My life turned into sixty-six years tonight.

384. Hey . . . You who lead Prayers: don't do what the heathens do.
Don't inject gibberish in the brains of simpleminded people.
And for your own benefits, don't dupe and weaken Iranians.
Who are lonely and afflicted; but highly respected.

385. Hey . . . Iranians: if you are willing to raise your overall status,
And for the good of your country you have high goals.
Burn the bushes of ignorance with the torch of logic
And defeat the tyrannical mullahs while you have a chance.

386. With true love and wisdom, a home does not differ from paradise.
Wealth does not assure our happiness or ends our anguish.
There are many wealthy who have two hundred sorrows.
While there are many unwealthy people whose hearts are empty of sadness.

387. The beloved demurs for her lover.
The lover sighs and moans of frustration.
While they are busy playing the game of avoiding and desiring,
Suddenly, Death Angel comes out of the ambush and says: "Let's go."

388. Hey . . . Mullahs: you should be impartially advised.
Your mentality is severely disturbed and needy of treatment.
But for the good of our country, and your own mental health,
Your thoughts, behavior, and sermons need medical intervention.

389. Hey . . . You Mullaist: you are obese like a pig,
And facially, you look like a toad.
Go and visit an experienced neurologist.
Who will tell you how hallow your brain is.

390. Those Iranians who had many grievances from the Shah,
And due to their fear and ignorance, they supported the Akhounds.
Now, frustrated with mullahs' regime, they regretfully and sadly
Keep describing Shah's justice, goodness and patriotism.

391. Hey . . . You who complain against the deceitful sheikhs
And tell us they are all full of tricks and frauds,
Even though you wear tie and hat in Europe,
You are yourself a mullah in thoughts, words, and action.

392. Hey . . . You who gave our country to the Arab-ridden mullahs,
Do you know what is the difference between you and I?
I am in love with my country but live in foreign land.
You live in Iran, but worship the Arab-minded foreigner.

393. Hey . . . You Army General: you are too far away from patriotism.
Don't insult and blame the mullahs and the Mullaists.
You are the one who breached your vows in defending our country,
But committed treason against our country and the Shah.

394. For many people, the Satan is the spiritual leader.
In many cases, the wolf is the shepherd of the sheep.
I have known many skillful physicians.
Who are, unfortunately, sicker than their Patients.

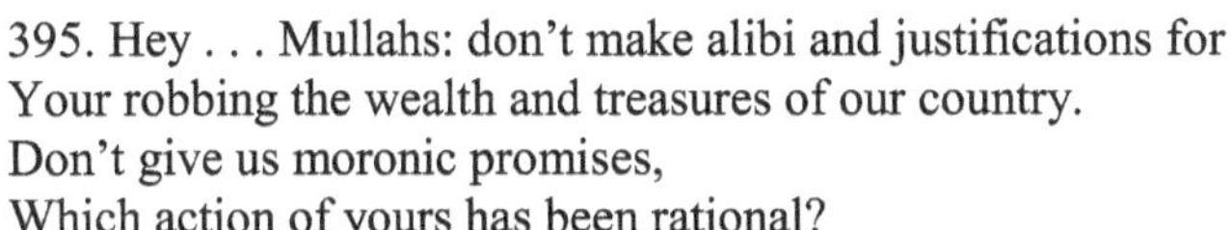

395. Hey . . . Mullahs: don't make alibi and justifications for
Your robbing the wealth and treasures of our country.
Don't give us moronic promises,
Which action of yours has been rational?

396. Sometimes, a smile is more stinging than an insult.
Sometimes, the value of a frown is more than coyness.
Sometimes, the eyes are expressive of lust and sensuality.
And sometimes, they are expressive of piety and purity.

397. Hey . . . You mullahs who live in Qum,
And as donkeys, you lack only tails.
If you don't have painful pebble in your shoes,
Why do you put them in the shoes of others?

398. Hey . . . You talented, well-tempered, and expressive poet,
You better realize the roles your poetic verses can play.
For the progress of our country, don't forget your responsibilities,
Which are necessary, valuable and effective.

399. Do you know why happiness has left our hearts
And why we worry about the future of our country and countrymen?
Because the lousy Akhounds whose income came from burial ceremony
Are now the members of Iranian parliament.

400. Hey . . . You, who wear a turban and a cloak
And always have the name of God on your tongue,
If you legalize prostitution under the name of temporary marriage,
Then, what is the difference between you and a pimp?

401. Hey . . . You Akhounds who are lost in a mirage
And blessed by Omar, you are the men of the Book (Quran).
Where God had said that: "The followers of Moses.
Deserve to be completely ruined and taken off the world's map?"

402. Oh . . . Iranians who have been deceived and duped by the mullahs,
You will never get bread out of their straws.
You got out of Shah's shallow hole with your feet,
But fell in mullahs' deep well with your head.

403. Religion is not the means by which you can be scientific.
Your predicaments will never be resolved by mullahs' idiocies.
Unfortunate are the regressive nations,
Whose governments are not separated from religion.

404. Although there is no signs of youth in my body
And there are no sorrows and enthusiasm of youth in my heart,
But although my heart longs for a global peace,
With the exception of love for Iran, nothing sparkles in my soul.

405. Oh . . . God: you have innumerable hajjis (those who went to Mecca).
And you prevail in the hearts of billions of people.
With all the power, glory and almightiness you possess.
Why do you need my obedience and prayer?

406. High bad cholesterol will not be treated by reciting the Holy Verses.
Mullahs will never be able to solve Iran's predicaments.
Sufism my friends, is not only incapable of solving our national problems.
It also misleads us to unreality, and ignores the objectivity of survival.

407. Hey . . . You base and ignorance-spreading mullahs,
From you, Iranians have gotten nothing except evil.
If under the name of concubine, you open up houses of prostitution,
Please decorate their entrances with your names and pictures.

408. Hey . . . You woman who have a son-in-law
And suffer from hives, gout and goiter,
Why you are pregnant at the age of fifty?
Have you lost your mind or you suddenly became insane?

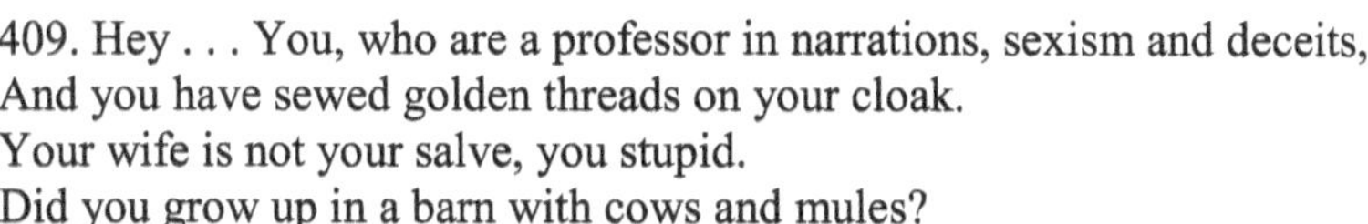

409. Hey . . . You, who are a professor in narrations, sexism and deceits,
And you have sewed golden threads on your cloak.
Your wife is not your salve, you stupid.
Did you grow up in a barn with cows and mules?

410. If your pains are more than your medicines,
Don't seek recovery from mullah or dervish.
Because if they could treat illnesses,
They could treat their own mental disorders.

411. If the mullahs start marketing prostitution under temporary marriage,
Don't be surprised, because they are all fornicators,
And they all approve your temporary marriage.
Because: under their turbans, they all wear the hats of pimps.

412. Hey . . . Mullahs: why you are denying the truth?
And insist that your delusions are correct?
If you are trying to seek the reality, learn scientific methods.
How long you repeat the unauthentic narrations and gibberish?

413. Hey . . . The Symbol of Evil: why are you against humanity for centuries?
And you are bloodthirsty, ignorant and impolite.
If you accuse "the Shah of being the servant of the West for few years,"
You have been the servant of Arabs for fourteen centuries.

414. The people who were Vazeers (ministers) during Shah's era.
And they severely backstabbed the country and the Shah.
Like mullahs, they committed treason against our country.
And now, they blame the "Great Satan" (the USA).

415. Oh . . . God: thank you for creating human.
And thank you also for creating the Earth, the oceans and the galaxies.
But, what were you motive, goal and need?
When you created Satan and the mullah?

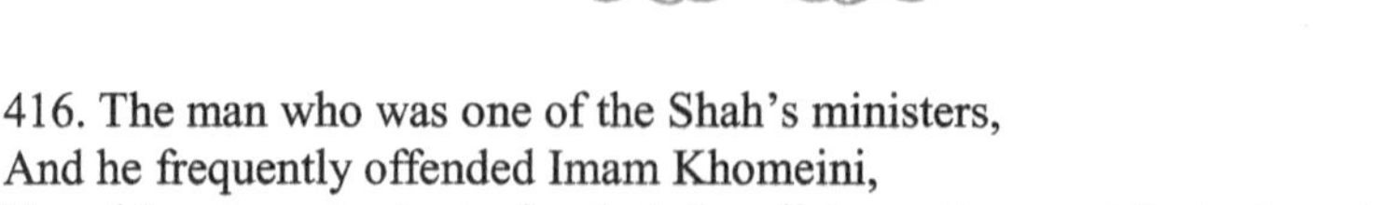

416. The man who was one of the Shah's ministers,
And he frequently offended Imam Khomeini,
He sold our country to Arab-minded mullahs, and now while in America,
He asserts that both Shah and Khomeini are ignorant.

417. Hey . . . Iranians: as long as your leader and government are dictatorial,
Your future will be very sorrowful and hopeless.
And as long as you are deprived of your human rights,
You and your country's conditions remain the same, or will get worse.

418. I have many flames of anguish in my heart.
My grief is now sixteen years old,
From the day God made me motherless.
I shed tears at dawns, and moan at nights.

419. Hey Moslems who seek prosperity by following God.
And for his cause you are willing to become a martyr.
Why then when you are praying to him
You raise your buttock toward him?

420. I don't know why I am so sad tonight,
And why I am in an angry mood with myself?
Neither poetry nor Quran makes me relaxed.
And even wine does not reduce my nostalgia.

421. As the Mullahs asserts, Mahdi (Shiite's Twelfth Imam) is still alive.
And with his capabilities, he will bring justice and stability.
I believe, however, that if Mahdi were alive and had any capability,
He had liberated himself from the bottom of the well.

422. Due to the ignorance that mullahs have hoarded in your brain.
Your intelligence is crippled and your reasons are rationally illogical.
Believing in fate, destiny, kismet, and the movement of stars,
Is the lesson that the mullahs have taught you for their own benefits.

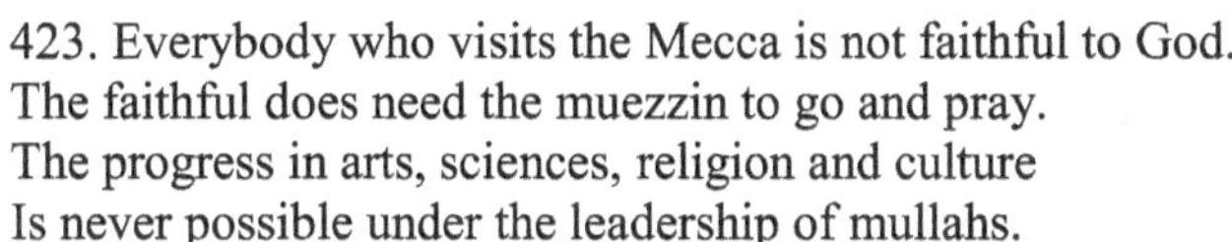

423. Everybody who visits the Mecca is not faithful to God.
The faithful does need the muezzin to go and pray.
The progress in arts, sciences, religion and culture
Is never possible under the leadership of mullahs.

424. Hey . . . You, who affirm, support and respect the mullahs,
For how long you bend in front of them?
Due to having respect, you bowed in front of the Shah.
But now due to your ignorance, you bow in front of the mullahs.

425. Hey you Arab-worshiping, misguided and foolish sheikhs,
When will you become aware of this truth and reality?
Iran has been the victim of religion for centuries.
Now you tell us that: "Shah of shahs was at fault"?

426. Hey . . . You sullen and treacherous Army General,
Why you are regretting what we had during Shah's reign.
It is you, who gave our country to the dictatorial Akhounds
And put our nation under current catastrophic circumstances.

427. Hey . . . Mullahs: you are so vulgar, blasphemous and asinine.
That bird-dropping is critical toward your wisdom and knowledge.
Your hair and beard certainly deserve the manure.
Because: you are still waiting for the appearance of the Absent Imam.

428. Hey . . . Iranians: move and don't be like statues.
Don't seek myths, and don't worship the dead.
The mullahs are the one who have blocked your way to progress.
Don't blame God, the West and the Lucifer.

429. Hey . . . you, who have been addicted to the sheikhs' idiocy,
Seek the causes of events through logic and sciences.
If the principle of cause-and-effects is beyond your intelligence,
Don't attribute them to fate, destiny and theological myths.

430. Hey . . . Moslem Clergies: don't terrify me of God.
Don't distort the truth by the inauthentic narrations.
If you are not capable of realizing the causes of natural phenomena,
Don't attribute the secrets of the universe to verses of the books.

431. Hey . . . Religious Leader: you are the most mischievous on the earth.
You are undoubtedly psychotic if you assume you are God-sent.
You are the one who has looted the wealth of our nation (Iran).
And you are the one who has put Iran under one hundred debts.

432. Oh . . . My dear Iranians: don't add to or exacerbate your calamities.
Don't doubt the truth of my poetic and patriotic advisements.
The mullahs have robbed your sense of reality and human rights.
Don't ever renew your contracts and promises with them.

433. Mullahs: the women's anguish is caused by your debauchery and stupidity.
Your insipidities are evident in your bragging and barking.
Spreading polygamy and temporary marriage under any names or rules
Indicate your pimping, sexist attitude and animalistic sexuality.

434. Hey . . . My Friends: don't listen to your uninformed heart.
Alert and motivate your lazy logic and rationality.
Instead of religious donations, fortunetelling and magic,
Solve your daily problems with science, intelligence and action.

435. Hey . . . Mullahs: don't doubt the goodness of God's deeds.
Without his prudence and approval nothing will takes place in the world.
If God was against the tragedy of Kerbela,
Hussein ibn Ali would not have been murdered by Yazid's troop.

436. My life passes through action; not just through talking.
It neither began from eternity nor will it exist after finality.
I am sixty-eight years old now, and with my connection with reality,
My life will passes through while I seek the gratification of my desires.

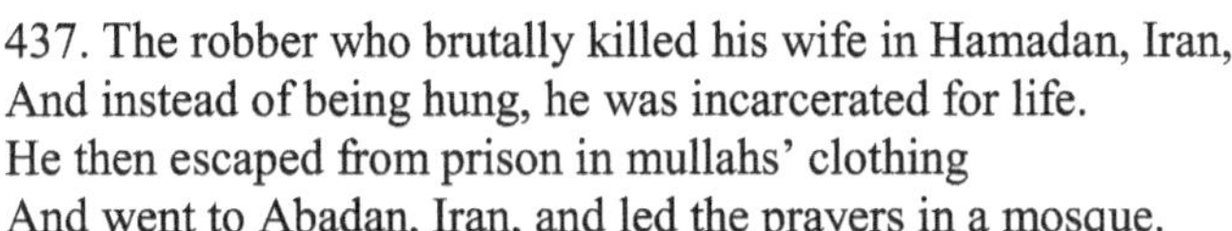

437. The robber who brutally killed his wife in Hamadan, Iran,
And instead of being hung, he was incarcerated for life.
He then escaped from prison in mullahs' clothing
And went to Abadan, Iran, and led the prayers in a mosque.

438. Hey . . . You who live next to the mosque
And your rosary has a hundred and one beads,
Why every night after praying at the sunset
You have the disposition of a drunk?

439. Oh . . . Iranians: who is concerned about our nation,
Who is following *Ahura Mazda*[72] or *Ahriman*[73],
Whoever tramples our human rights, either shah or sheikh
Is, undoubtedly, our foe and the enemy of our nation.

440. From the free-loading and unworthy Akhounds,
Never expect intelligence and truthfulness.
Because if Ali, the First Imam, was the Lion of God.
The Akhounds are, due to their stupidity, the Donkeys of God.

441. Hey . . . You Superstitious, Moronic and Rigid-Minded Akhound,
Except torture, what the patriotic writers have received from you?
In loving our country you, like former turbaned leader,
Came out to be worse that a lemon.

442. Hey . . .You, who follow the path of mullahs,
Do you know the mullahs plays with your gullible head like a ball?
Your weakness, anguish, anxiety, regression and superstitious beliefs,
Are the assets, goals, hopes and sources of income for Mullahs.

72: *Ahura Mazda:* God in Zoroastrian Religion.

73: *Ahriman:* Satan in Zoroastrian Religion.

443. The mullahs say: "On the first night in our graves.
Two *Angels*[74] enter our graves forcefully.
And after they ask us some questions about Islam,
They leave our graves impatiently."

444. Hey . . . Iranians: how long you want to be sad worshiping the dead?
How long you want your hands tied up at the pleasurable table of life?
How long you let the mullahs to afflict you with their hyper-religiosity?
How long you want to tolerate the tyranny and autocracy of the Akhounds?

445. Oh . . . My friends: don't get angry with the bitterness of the truth.
There is a difference between science and incantation.
Contrary to the narrations, Holy Verses and the absurd myths,
Scientifically, however, you have evolved from the apes.

446. Oh . . . Iran: your bright dawns are darkened by mullahs' smoky deceits.
The worsening of your sorrows is due to Khomeini's arrival.
Your freedom of thoughts, rational deeds and speech are obtainable,
Provided you free yourself from mullahs' pathological rigidities.

447. Hey . . . You Prayer Leader: don't bend your body.
Don't pollute the air of the mosque with your filthy odor.
For the benefit of whoever prostrate behind you,
Wash your bottom instead of performing ablution.

448. Hey . . . Iranians: who is concerned about your future?
Who is responsible to help you to develop your creative minds?
Take the leash of mullahs off your neck,
The pearl of art and science becomes you much better.

---

74 *Angels:* Nakir and Munker are two angels who enter one's grave on the first night of her/his burial for the purpose of asking her/him: Who is her/his God? What is her/his Religion? And who is her/his prophet?

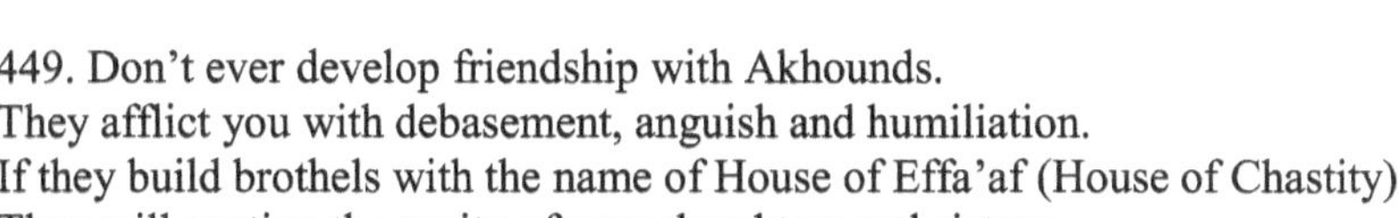

449. Don't ever develop friendship with Akhounds.
They afflict you with debasement, anguish and humiliation.
If they build brothels with the name of House of Effa'af (House of Chastity)
They will auction the purity of your daughters and sisters.

450. Hey . . . You, who performed the hajj rituals in Mecca,
And now you are a refugee in America.
With the exception of looting the wealth of our country, Iran,
Where did you get your uncountable wealth from?

451. There are many people who are more innocent than Imam Hussein.
There are many who are more deprived of bread and water than he was.
There are many ill, hungry and sick orphans.
Who are more innocent than the two sons of Imam Hussein.

452. The self-praising man who worshiped himself,
And he overestimated his lovemaking skills.
Due to the fear of his poor sexual performance,
He wetted himself on his wedding night.

453. Hey . . . You traitor, hireling and deceitful Akhounds,
Why have you been asking God to destroy the Western nations?
You are worse than the West, and the real enemy of Iran.
In Arabic, the difference between the West and Arab is only one dot.

454. The sheikh who presents sermons against corruption and undercutting,
And he asserts that martyrs will go to paradise on the day of resurrection.
With bribery and testicle-rubbing (ass-kissing),
He exempted his two sons form mandatory participation in Iran-Iraq war.

455. The Mullah who teaches chastity and purity lessons,
And he goes to Mecca every year.
A week after his wife passed away,
He slept with a harlot in the city of Qum.

456. Do you know why you are poor and sorrowful
And you are deprived of your human rights, wisdom and happiness?
Because every step you take forward on mullahs' path,
You take one hundred steps backward and away from realities.

457. Hey . . . You, who have sacrificed your intelligence for religious myths
And have no knowledge about the ocean, the earth and galaxies,
How can you, with few narrations and Holy Verses
Explain the creation of universe and its nature?

458. Do you know why you have many problems and sorrows
And you have no job, no food, nothing to drink and nowhere to reside?
Because instead of using wisdom in solving your earthly problems.
You, illogically, worry about your future in the invisible world.

459. The Akhoundeotic person who was obese like an elephant
And said: "A lot of warts have grown on his testicles."
Instead of seeking medical treatment, every Friday night,
He puts a monetary donation on the grave of the ayatollah.

460. Hey . . . You Lazy Mullah, who were born out of wedlock
And except the ridiculous narrations, no literacy pours out of your mouth,
If you claim to be a devoted and blessed Moslem,
Then why you yourself don't go to jihad (Islamic holy war)?

461. The mullah whose savagery is worse than the caveman's
And had sex with a foal for three years,
He violated *Imam Khomeini's Order*[75] by selling the foal
To another mullah who lived in his hometown.

75: Imam Khomeini's Order: According to this order, if a Moslem man has sexual relation with a donkey and decides to sell it, he is prohibited to sell it in his hometown (quoted from Tauzeeh-ul-Masail, Authored by Imam Khomeini).

462. The Akhound who, in violation of Islamic law, was greedy
And his insanity had severely elapsed.
He suddenly divorced his wife, and
Bought a female goat; he is now is a zoophillic.

463. Hey . . . You, who drip saliva out of your mouth
Every time you see food on the stove,
Eat less, eat better, and exercise.
Being skinny and healthy is better than being obese and ill.

464. Oh . . . God: be generous to my country (Iran).
And take this unchaste religious leader to your hell soon.
Would you please help Iran and Iranians
By endowing other mullahs with humanitarianism and objectivity?

465. The mullah who claims to have a holy halo around his skull
And deceitfully covers up every mistake the Supreme Leader makes.
Since he was himself sexually abused,
He has temporarily married a girl who is only ten years old.

466. Hey . . . Friends: don't let my laughter misleads you.
Or my happy appearance deceives you.
I am afraid if I tell you about my anguishes.
You may start shedding tears for me.

467. A devoted Moslem who arrived in a hotel in Austria,
He entered the restroom to use the toilet.
But since the toilet seat was built facing the *Qiblah*[76],
He did not use it, and polluted his front and back with filth.

76: ***Qiblah:*** Mecca, toward which all Moslems should not expose their privates or sit on the toilets facing it. In addition, prayers should be performed facing Mecca, and the deceased should be also buried facing it.

468. The mullahs make more mistakes than their Supreme Leader.
They are hundred times more shortsighted than him.
There are many ten-year -old children, who are more informed
About what goes on around the world than these insipid Mullahs.

469. Hey . . . You Iranians: don't accuse the West of exploiting you.
The mullahs are the ones who have robbed you of your right to live freely.
As long as you are far away from sciences, human rights and positive action
You will be a puppet in the hands of other nations.

470. Oh . . . My Dear Iran: when will you become self-sufficient?
When you will be free of anguish and calamities?
Let us assume you free yourself from the influence of the West,
When will you free yourself from the evil of the Akhounds?

471. Do you know why your difficulties don't become simple,
And your soul will not be freed of pains and sorrows?
Akhoundeosis is the root of your mental problems,
And will never be treated by divine messages.

472. Hey . . . Immigrants: if America is paying your expenses and feed you,
And it also pays your physicians and pharmacist,
Why, then, instead of appreciating its generosity and civilities
You have hundred stupid criticisms and grievances against it?

473. Hey . . . You man who Committed Adultery
And have no notions of shame and dignity,
Your ignorance and hypocrisy have become so intense
That you are now claiming chastity in the mosque.

474. There are some rabbis who are like mullahs.
There are more prejudiced Catholic priests than Jewish preachers.
There are many followers of other major religions in the world
Who are less foolish and disturbed than the prayer-leading Akhounds.

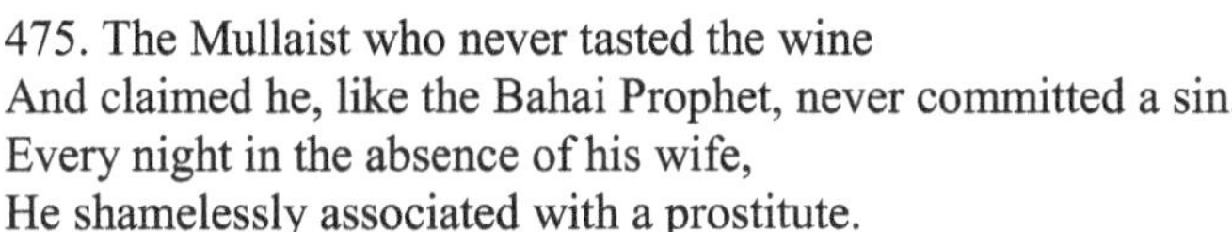

475. The Mullaist who never tasted the wine
And claimed he, like the Bahai Prophet, never committed a sin.
Every night in the absence of his wife,
He shamelessly associated with a prostitute.

476. The Iranian professor who had Mullaistic mentality.
And while in Qum, he always wrote against the West.
Now while in the US, he receives monthly payment from US government.
He keeps saying: "America is better than the Garden of Eden."

477. If, as you keep saying, you don't like America
And say Americans are mean and selfish,
Then why you are trying to be a US citizen?
And to meet its citizenship requirements you pay for its expenses?

478. The man who got drunk and severely wounded his wife
And he visited the brothels once in a week,
I saw him having Akhoundeotic symptoms
When he was teaching his daughter how to be pure and chaste.

479. How long you keep sleeping with your seven-faced husband?
And like a salve, you clean the house and tolerate pain?
Earn your rights from your Mullahistic husband.
How long you want to suffer and take medications?

480. Hey . . . Religious Leader: shut up and zip up your lips.
Except corruption, what else have you done for Iran?
Why did you reproach Ferdowsi?
I hope God will cut off your tongue.

481. Hey . . . Mullahs: you kicked the shah out of the country
Because you believed he befriended the Western leaders.
The real traitors are you, who like your former caliphs,
Have misled and fooled many civilized nations like Egypt and Persia.

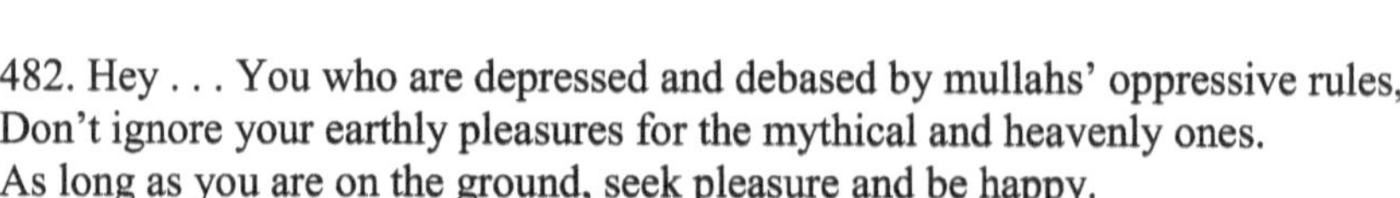

482. Hey . . . You who are depressed and debased by mullahs' oppressive rules,
Don't ignore your earthly pleasures for the mythical and heavenly ones.
As long as you are on the ground, seek pleasure and be happy.
And don't forget that finally you will be under the ground.

483. Moses who became a prophet by the order of God,
And he brought us the Ten Commandments as God's gifts.
Why with his countless miraculous capabilities
He spent forty years to reach the Promised Land?

484. Don't lie and tell me you believe in the monotheistic books.
You sound like you live in a mirage, like the mullahs.
As long as you have no deterministic contact with the realities of life,
You are full of pains, anguishes, and tribulations.

485. Do you know why your sorrows don't decrease?
And your mental symptoms don't go away with therapy and drugs?
Because as long as you identify with and imitate the Akhounds,
Your condition will not be better than that of an ape.

486. The seekers of the truth doubt whatever the mullahs say and do.
Only a fool expects the willow trees will bear any grapes.
The Mullaists are those who blindly and unquestionably.
Imitate the prayer leader of their towns.

487. If your perceptions are reality-oriented,
Your mind becomes clean of the sorrows of life and fear of death.
Every living thing, finally, like you and I my friend,
Becomes inanimate and turns into dust.

488. Since our country (Iran) has been sacrificed for the profits of Akhounds.
Ignorance, rates of death, prostitution and poverty have gravely increased.
But if the prices of eggs, cheese and meat have drastically gone up,
The prices of turban, sandals, and Abba (Islamic cloak) have been reduced.

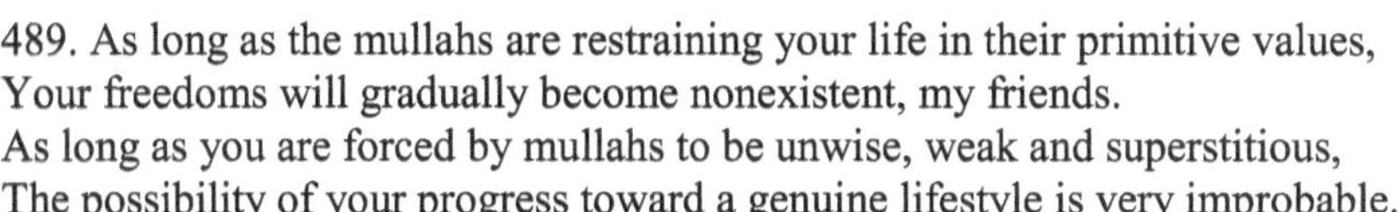

489. As long as the mullahs are restraining your life in their primitive values,
Your freedoms will gradually become nonexistent, my friends.
As long as you are forced by mullahs to be unwise, weak and superstitious,
The possibility of your progress toward a genuine lifestyle is very improbable.

490. Hey . . . You Girl who live in the house next to mine,
And you know I am home because my lights are on,
Why you don't drop by and ask myself how I am doing?
But you keep asking our neighbors how I am?

491. Many people are running toward God.
And many are running away from Lucifer.
But if you look at them deeply and realistically, you will find out
That God and Satan are both within them.

492. Your foresight is blind because the mullahs have polluted your mentality.
Your fears guarantee the existence and operations of the mullahs.
The fears of death, hell and God the clergies have injected in your mind
Are indicative of your unrealistic insight, which is the source of their income.

493. The priest who directed a church
And he devoted his life to teaching what Jesus said and did,
He became incarcerated because he sexually abused children.
When I saw him in his jail cell, he was asking Moses for forgiveness.

494. As long as the Mullaists are running our country, my friends,
The bases of our government are snakes' pits.
All religions are, in one way or another,
Afflicted with the parasitic attributes of their leaders.

495. From the moment that Arabs crossed the boundary of our country,
They have Arabized our elegant language.
Since the rise of Islam, the Arab-stricken mullahs
Have been brainwashing our countrymen with their superstitions and myths.

496. The Nun who was pure like the Holy Book
And she had never committed a sin,
She committed suicide by overdose on the altar.
Because: She was raped by the priest.

497. Hey . . . Mullahs: You have rotten thoughts.
And you are thousand steps below the status of a genuine sage.
If you have collected few documents against the Shah,
God has collected thousands documents against you.

498. There are many heretics who are in heaven.
There are many ruthless who are the jurists.
There are many murderers and traitors, who in the name of religion,
Are free, wealthy, and have high positions.

499. Hey . . . Akhounds: don't ransack the wealth of Iran.
Don't spread the seeds of grieving by your ignorance.
You are undoubtedly a traitor and brutal terrorist
Who has deprived our nation of her Human Rights.

500. There are many women who are superior to men.
There are many men who are afraid of women.
The Akhounds who degrade the value of women,
Are like donkeys without tails and saddles.

501. There are many smiling people who are crying inside.
There are many *people who have teeth but have no bread to eat*[77].
There are many hajjis, rabbi, priests and pastors
Who serve Lucifer instead of God.

502. The Christian mother who has done many good for her mankind,
And she has written few books about child-rearing strategies.
I saw her, instead of washing her filthy child,
She was washing her dog with soap and rosewater.

---

*77: **An Iranian Proverb:*** "Whoever (the Creator) gives the teeth also gives the food."

503. The nun who was obsessively addicted to prayers.
And billed and cooed with the portrait of Jesus
Told me: "There are many nuns and priests."
Who are, like herself, "homosexual in the world."

504. Mullahs: your path is darker than the bottom of the deep well.
Dogs have much better temperament than you do.
There are many non-Moslems who, in their hearts,
Are more faithful to God than the residents of Mecca.

505. Oh . . . Iranians: don't make the sorrows of my heart overflow.
Don't say bad things about the residents of *Rasht*[78] and *Tabriz*[79].
Stop ridiculing your countrymen and begin to respect them.
And don't lose your love for your country.

506. In playing the games of life, I am not a looser.
Of serving the needy people, I am not tired.
If I am summoned on the day of resurrection,
I will not be disgraced in front of God.

507. Zahrah who fought for the women's right in Iran
And criticized the religious leader for his sexist teachings,
She was beheaded by the order of the Akhounds,
Who announced that: "She became shahid (martyr) in the cause of God."

508. Hey . . . You Iranian Ladies: don't dress up like Arab women.
Don't make your life troublesome with palmistry and superstitions.
If the disease of Akhoundeosis has made you a mental patient,
Don't complain of God, your husband and destiny.

78: *Rasht:* A city on Northern Iran.

79: *Tabriz:* A city in Northwestern Iran.

509. Hey Mullah Jennati80: you are a shame in Islamic traditions.
Your mind has been poisoned with many prejudices.
With the severe hostility you have toward women.
You will be, indeed, in hell but not in *Jennat*[81].

510. Realism makes you free of your pains and sorrows.
It enhances your problem-solving skills.
Belief in superstitions deprives you of deterministic principles
And will afflict you with the diseases of ignorance and anguish.

511. The sheikh who has madly fallen in love with the Arabic creeds
And has imprisoned those who love our country (Persia),
Says: "If" he is "atrocious, evil and foolish,
God has created" him "this way."

512. The Mullaist who had no respect for medical sciences
Became sick, but never took his prescribed medicines.
But when he prayed by the grave of an imam's descendant for recovery,
He never recovered, and died of ignorance and high fever.

513. Hey . . . Mullah: if you have honor and chastity,
And as you claim, you are purer than the sacred,
Then, why in protecting the chastity of our country (Iran),
You have no zeal; you commit treason and are a hypocrite?

514. Those who have been governing our country after the Shah
And destroyed whatever we had gained toward modernity,
They drowned close to ten thousand innocent people in blood.
Now they say: Their "victims were sinful and impure like the Shah."

80: Jennati: An Iranian Ayatollah who is pathologically prejudiced against women; he is a sick sexist.

81: Jennat: Paradise in Arabic language. Thus, Jennati refers to anyone who is or will be a resident of paradise.

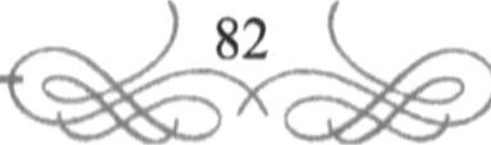

515. The sheikh who leads the prayer in the mosque,
And in his little private shop he sells stupidity.
Like his moronic leader, instead of medications,
He hops that praying at the grave of the chief mullah will cure him.

516. Hey Ayatollah Karroobi: you are, indeed, the source of deceptions.
Don't praise Khalkhali who murdered hundreds of innocent Iranians.
Without the doubt, like the murderers of Imam Hussein's children,
You are related to the clan of Yazid.

517. Those who, are oppressed by the tyranny of the mullahs
Are countless in the world my friends.
Akhoundeosis does not only prevail in Islam.
All religions are inflicted with this disorder in one way or other.

518. Hey . . . You who believe in the intelligence of Mullah Khomeini
And keep saying that he is the professor of all virtues,
If you want to know about his ignorance and primitiveness,
Read his books entitles: Tauzeeh-ul-Masail and Tahrir al-Wasilah.

519. Hey . . . Iranians: You have retrograded by the oppression of mullahs.
And have lost to them your human rights and freedom you had gained.
Did you know this renegade government spent millions of Dollars.
Out of your wealth, to build a gravesite for the fake Imam Khomeini?

520. Hey . . . You bazaries (working in bazaars), professors and military men,
What about the mullah were better than those of the Shah?
If you had read the absurd and sordid books of the Fake Imam,
You would never have entitled and chosen him as a leader.

521. Hey . . . Mullahs: don't corrupt and weaken the government.
Don't torture and imprison innocent Iranians in the name of religion.
The weakness of our country is profitable for other countries.
Stop being a traitor and negligent; don't force our nation to regress.

522. The akhound, who due to your immaturity, has become your ruler
Neither loves your nation nor does he respect you.
He is thirsty for power, fame, wealth and status.
His overall gratifications are dependent on your deprivations.

523. Hey . . . You Supreme Leader: your sermons are void of truth and reality.
Your deed is indicative of your defiance against God's humanitarianism.
Your democidal crimes and terrorism under the name of religion
Are the signs of savagery, lack of patriotism and primitive ruling skills.

524. Hey . . . Mullah: your disorder is due to your pathological closed-mindedness.
Your idiocy is the sign of your decayed and rotten doctrine.
Killing the country's youths to maintain your theocracy
Is the sign of your insanity, depravity and animalistic nature.

525. Hey . . . You Akhounds: deceiving is your never-ending deed.
We know wheedling the simpleminded guarantees your occupation.
For centuries, the pains, sorrows and weakness of Iranians have been
The outcome of your religious dictatorship and primitive mentality.

526. The Mullaist professor who taught physics
And was a participant in killing the Iranian youths
Told me in my office: "I will not get sexually turned on,
If my wife do not spits on my face several times."

527. Come on Man: don't sadden your wife with your sarcasm.
Don't degrade her in the presence of your mother.
Don't teach your son superstitions and delusions.
And don't make your daughter tearful by putting her down.

528. If you rationally view the Mullaists who are currently ruling our nation,
You will realize that they are using you as mule for their rides.
Religions that survive on human blood are based on:
Stupidity, brutality, animosity, intolerance and lack of patriotism.

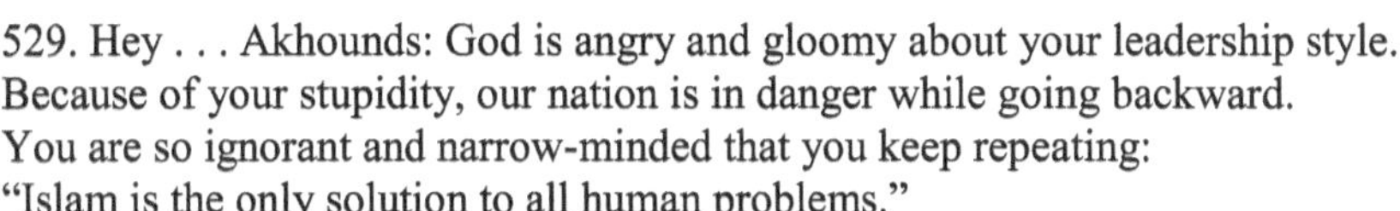

529. Hey . . . Akhounds: God is angry and gloomy about your leadership style.
Because of your stupidity, our nation is in danger while going backward.
You are so ignorant and narrow-minded that you keep repeating:
"Islam is the only solution to all human problems."

530. Hey . . . You, who have the Potentials for Becoming a Genius,
When you will reach the maturity of your intelligence?
Your potential talents will never be actualized and developed.
As long as the Akhounds are opposed to sciences by narrations.

531. The Akhoundeotic military captain who lived in Qum
And he had sex with the daughter of a chief mullah.
Since he had not followed the rules of having a concubine,
Afraid of her father, he left Qum in women's clothing.

532. Hey . . . You who have, pains, suffering and distractions,
Drinking alcohol will never heal your problems.
The reasons for your disturbed eating and sleeping patterns are.
Depression, anxiety and morbidity.

533. Hey . . . You who only finished dabista'n (grade school):
You are so misled that aiming for the Mecca, you ended up in *Lorestan*[82].
How do you dare without any literary background and knowledge?
Make criticisms of Sa'di's *Gulistan*[83]?

534. If you have anguish, tears and fatigue
And get only little pleasure out of life and love,
If your physician has said you are bodily healthy,
Then your illness is clinical depression.

82: *Loresta'n:* A Western Iranian province. The whole sentence is an Iranian adage referring to an individual who is misled and has lost his orientation due to mental disturbance.

83: *Gulistan:* A poetic volume versed by Sa'di, who is one of the legends in classic Iranian poetry.

535. The . . . Mullaist who owns six rented houses,
And although he has come back from hajj, he does not follow God's rules.
He, in his attempt to steal his wife's property with trick,
He wanted me to write his wife is insane with impaired judgment.

536. The nation (Iran) is now more heartsick than in Shah's era.
Hey . . . Mullah: there are many robbers who are less greedy than you are.
The number of the crimes you have committed in Iran
Are thousands times more than the threads of hair in your bushy beard.

537. Every mojtahed (jihad-ordering mullah) steals your mind and wealth.
Like Yazid, he deprives you of what you need to live on.
Don't relax with the hope that one of these days, the mullahs
Will realize your worth or return your human rights.

538. If you are in love with my looks and temperament,
Why sometimes you publicly disrespect me?
If, as you claim, I am always in your heart,
Then, why you are looking for me, my dear?

539. Happy are those who eat and drink their own bread and wine.
And make rosewater out of their own garden's flowers.
Intelligent people are those who prior to their last one-way journey
Clean their financial deals with others.

540. If your leader were not so rich in ignorance.
Yours and your country's circumstances were not so disastrous.
And if he faithfully believed in the day of resurrection,
He could not be, like the mullahs, so offensive, bloodthirsty and sinful.

541. Oh . . . My Friends: try to protect your territory and boundary,
Attempt to manage your own affairs intelligently.
If you are seeking a long and healthy life,
Listen to what I and your physician tell you.

542. I adore your beautiful and questioning eyes.
I love your blossom-looking and kiss-seeking lips.
I beg you, come on and sit next to me.
So I can kiss your lips, eyes and gorgeous face.

543. Hey . . . Mullah: You are an Arab-worshiping impostor and a thief.
You have no knowledge of scientific governmental strategies.
With all of your atrocities, sinfulness and oppressiveness,
How will you answer to God's questions on the doomsday?

544. Hey . . . You stupid, blasphemous, and garrulous Akhounds,
We don't need your narrations and sermons anymore.
If you are afraid of God, we are afraid of falsehood.
While we are seeking the truth, you are on the rout to Ka'bah.

545. Hey . . . Sheikh who hated the Shah and make money by praying on corpse,
And you are homicidal, thief, treacherous and sinful.
If you really believe in the existence of heaven and hell,
Why do you keep breaking God's rules and advices?

546. Hey . . . You Mean Sheikh: you are the true symbol of the devil.
Like Goliath, you are animalistic and godless.
You are the one, who for the purpose of destruction and terrorism
Give the psychotic blasphemous terrorists money and weapon.

547. Hey . . . You Priest who polluted the cross with your sins
And with sexually abusing children you violated Christ's doctrine.
The life sentence does not cleanse your sins.
If you want to really repent, you better cut off your testicles.

548. Hey . . . My Friends: don't torment your beloved.
In dealing with her/him, don't lose your patience.
If you have problems with yourself or your beloved,
Listen to me and your physician's recommendations.

549. Try to justly obtain your share out of life.
Surpass your competitors with your intelligence.
If you don't want to be financially broke.
Don't lose sight of how much cash you have.

550. Hey . . . Sheikhs: The priests are as sinful as you are.
Like them, you are mentally disturbed and lack zeal.
The priests sexually abuse members of their congregation.
You deflower adolescent girls as concubines.

551. I wish wisdom was an international attribute,
And it was also the pillar and wealth of life.
I wish in keeping the peace among the nations,
There were sympathy, respect, humanitarianism and trust.

552. Hey . . . Iranians: don't let mullahs' prayers deceive you.
Your dumbness satisfies mullahs' motives.
Mullahs have ransacked whatever valuable you had.
For how long you are going to be dancing to mullahs' tune?

553. The man who was a merchant of turbans and cloaks
And his wife, afraid of getting killed by him, divorced him.
Iranian court of law decided that he was not guilty because
He "killed" his "daughter following the order of God" (honor killing).

554. The woman who changed her Arabic name into Persian name
And she was the concubine of a vulgar Mullaist in Qum.
Now while she resides in Irvine, California,
She goes to a ballet class every day.

555. I wish my soul was free of sorrows,
And I was free of the anguish about my country.
I wish in calming down my painful nostalgia.
I had an effective ointment beside wine and poetry.

556. My adorable beloved: I wish there were a next world,
And in it, there were libraries, music halls, bars and cupbearers.
I wish for me and you in that world, my dear.
There will be a room, a kitchen and a bed.

557. While evaluating an Iranian man in prison
Who was accused of purchasing a stolen car,
I asked him: How was he doing in being jailed?
He said: He is "better treated here than under the Akhound's regime."

558. The Iranian woman who wore the veil and was the symbol of modesty in Iran.
She came to Newport Beach, California few months ago.
Once I saw her in bikini on the beach.
As soon as she saw me seeing her, she dived in the water.

559. Although I don't "cut the moon in half" as Prophet Muhammad did,
I would not loosen the intellectual foundation in mankind.
Your religious leaders are dumber than you are.
And I will not lose my mind by following dumb religious leaders.

560. Don't hoard food in your body my friend.
Don't get obese and make your walking through life problematic.
By eating the things that only satisfy your cravings,
Don't make your heart, liver and kidney sick.

561. The woman who was heartbroken by her husband's meanness,
But she lived with him only for the sake of her child.
I asked her: "What is the difference between you and Eve?"
She said: "Nothing, except her husband was Adam" (human in Farsi).

562. The mullah-ridden man who came to US from Zarand, Iran,
And he suffered severely from diabetic symptoms.
He ate honey and dates with his breakfast every morning
And kept saying: "It is God's will that I have diabetes."

563. Hey . . . You Mullahs: you have no virtue.
Why you are not afraid of God's punitive action?
You are the one who deceitfully shows wheat but sell barley.
You are also the one who has no decree except murdering and deceitfulness.

564. Hey you Supreme Leader who, like a mule, are giving ride to Satan,
And your stupidity is the cause of Iran's pain and sadness.
When you leave this world, without a doubt,
God will punish you most severely in hell.

565. Those who sacrificed you for their own benefits
And feel proud because they made a revolution,
If you intelligently look at every aspect of your life,
You will see they have polluted your life with their filthy thoughts and deeds.

566. Don't assume that whoever wears a turban,
He is virtuous, infallible and sinless.
There are many turbans wearers who are pledged to Satan,
And under their turbans, they have hidden the brains of donkeys

567. Hey . . . You late Fake Imam: you were certainly wicked and ignorant,
And you ruled Iran under the names of religion and God.
You murdered at least one hundred college students.
I hope dogs will defecate on your grave.

568. If you have migraine headache or your fontanel lobe hurts.
Fish meat and ginger are your best recovery agents.
And if your level of iron has gone down,
Eat spinach several times per week.

569. The sheikh's son who worshiped the wine
And his heart and faith were devoted to the bar's cupbearer
One night his father told him: "Don't ever go to the bars."
The son replied: "Will you ever stop going to the mosque?"

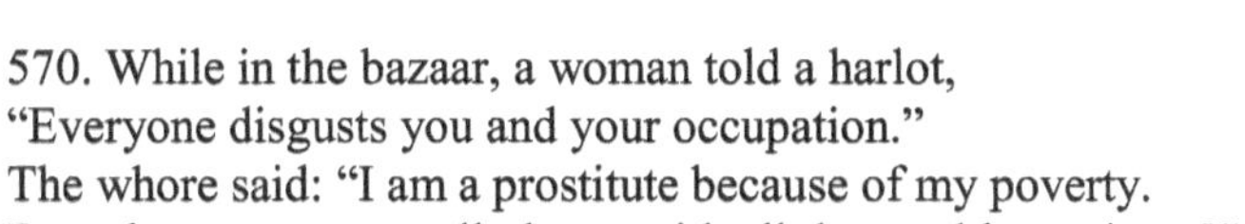

570. While in the bazaar, a woman told a harlot,
"Everyone disgusts you and your occupation."
The whore said: "I am a prostitute because of my poverty.
But why are you sexually loose with all the wealth you have?"

571. Hey . . . Man: if you claim you know how to compromise,
You better be modest if you want to strengthen your marital ties.
It is ugly and idiotic if you put down your wife in the presence of others.
So, never insult your wife privately or publicly if you are wise.

572. The sheikh who has faith in the invisibles
And his veins and arteries are full of Arab's blood,
He claims that he has seen Mahdi, the Absent Imam.
But from a clinical perspective, he has delusion and hallucination.

573. Hey . . . You who due to ignorance rip your chest with dragon.
And for Imam Husain, you pour dust on your head.
Every time you go to the mosque to pray,
Please cleanse your body of stench.

574. Hey . . . You, who are a respectable physician,
And your specialty is pulmonary diseases.
Why you are always smoking cigarette?
Even, while you are dancing?

575. If you want to live a long healthy life.
Exercise every morning before you pray.
And if your blood fat has reached two hundred,
Enjoy eating garlic, nuts and onions.

576. Hey Mullahs: you are all far away from the truth and reality,
And opposed to sciences, you are drowned in superstitions.
Be sure that the floods, earthquakes, plague and cholera
Are all the effects of natural causes, not God's angers.

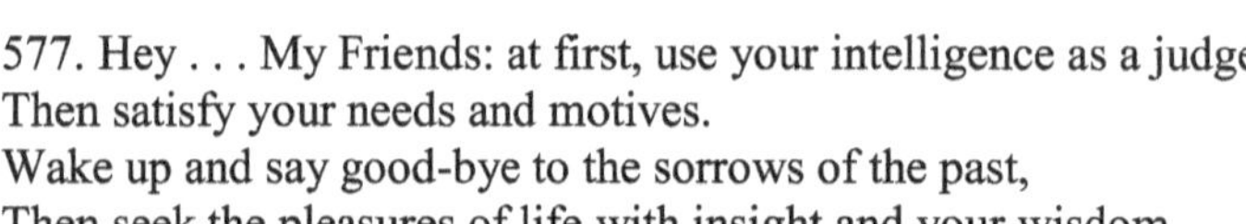

577. Hey . . . My Friends: at first, use your intelligence as a judge,
Then satisfy your needs and motives.
Wake up and say good-bye to the sorrows of the past,
Then seek the pleasures of life with insight and your wisdom.

578. Hajji Ramadan, who came to the US from Saraab, Iran
And was against prostitution, wine-drinking and the "wicked West."
He married a prostitute who was French,
And she was chronically addicted to alcohol.

579. Those who sacrificed our country for religion
And claimed they have a high status in God's court,
For the purpose of spreading ignorance and superstitions,
They have opened up two hundred mosques and Madresahs (Schools) in Iran.

580. I wish mankind were free of discords and hostility.
And he wear free of barbaric characters.
I wish mankind, instead of accepting the mullahs' doctrine,
He had faith in humanitarian principles.

581. Hey . . . You Mullah: you don't have the tiniest idea of the truth.
And you have never tasted the electuary of wisdom.
Why last night while sermonizing on the pulpit,
You claimed you belong to the truthful group?

582. Oh you whose wealth and creditability have been robbed by the Mullahs,
Don't ever doubt that they have darkened your path to the pleasures of life.
Alas, you are the one, who allowed the deceitful mullahs
Use you like donkey to ride on toward their regressive goals.

583. The woman whose color changes of shame when she sees an unknown man
And she is so religious that she covers her hair when a rooster looks at her,
Under the veils of chastity, modesty and bashfulness, however,
She does the things that even a harlot will feel ashamed to do.

584. Hey you mullahs, who are severely deprived of arts, sciences and civility.
How long you want to suffer the pain and anguish of ignorance?
If you want to get rid of the symptoms of your primitive absurdities,
Go forward; why you are going backward to fourteen centuries ago?

585. The lady who was depressed of being apart from her husband
And she came to the US from Qazvin, Iran.
As soon as she received her green card,
She divorced her husband and got his car.

586. Hey . . . Mullah: a moronic leader like you is rare in this era.
Your *Tauzeeh-ul-Masail*[84] is the evidence of your mental illness.
One half of this book contains primitive absurdities,
And the other half is about the organs below the belly.

587. Do you know why you have become depressed?
And you have lost hopes in yourself, life and recovery?
Because instead of seeking and experiencing pleasure here on earth.
You have faith in paradise and the services of its Houris and Ghelmans.

588. Mullah: you are more of a stranger to Iran than the East and the West.
You are more absurdly talkative than your deceased leader.
I have seen three thousand insane patients in my career,
But you are much more insane than all of them.

589. As long as your government is contaminated with hyper-religiosity,
You and your country will be under the same problematic circumstances.
Your helplessness, anguishes and backwardness
Are caused by your leader's ignorance, from which the West benefits.

590. Does everyone who has a good figure and is beautiful or handsome
Is wise, intelligence, mature, and healthy?
There are many unattractive people who are highly intelligent,
And there are many attractive people who are deprived of wisdom.

84: *Tauzeeh-ul-Masail (Problems-Explanations):* Written by Rohollah Khomeini and published by Ismaelian publisher, in Tehran, Iran. No date indicated.

591. Hey . . . Sheikhs: your doctrine does not have intellectual foundation.
Your long and bushy hairs are not the criterion of genuine religiosity.
Your thievery, deceitfulness and charlatanism under the name of God
Are not the right paths toward humanitarian lifestyle.

592. Don't ever seek appeasement from the Akhounds.
They don't know the meaning of sympathy and compassion.
Thus, by following their absurd, misleading and nonsensical creeds,
Don't go through life with vanity, idleness and bewilderment.

593. Do you know why mullahs' mules are stuck in the deep mud?
Because, the loads of their riders' superstitions are extremely heavy.
Do you know why mullahs are afraid of taking their turbans off?
Because they are terrified that reality will enter into their minds.

594. Hey Woman: you moan because you are a busy housewife and mother.
And you tell me you are "not so happy with your marriage."
Then, why at the age of forty with five children,
You are pregnant, contrary to the advices of me and your gynecologist?

595. Among many hidden and vivid stars in the galaxies,
Only one star may become the sun.
And out of the innumerable drops of rain,
Only one drop turns into pearl in a shell.

596. Why you are so preoccupied with the problems in upper world?
When you will be thinking about your problems here on earth?
Although you are theoretically the servant of God,
But practically, the clergies have made you their own slaves.

597. I will not follow the religion of the ridiculous priests.
And I will not believe in their miracles of treating the sick.
And about the hell, which they have built themselves,
I would not let my soul to experience stress.

598. A child is like a flower, and his home is like a flowerpot.
There are many homes which are worse than prisons.
The slow-growing, the blossomless and withering of flowers
Are caused by their poor environment and the negligence of gardeners.

599. The mullahs' goals are to make you feel guilty, afraid and mentally insecure.
They are your first enemies, and the West may be your second foe.
Having faith in Naker and Monker, and the *Bridge of Sirat*[85],
Are the absurdities they have taught you and, from which, they make money.

600. A sheikh asked a beautiful and gorgeously figured woman,
"Would you like to be temporarily or permanently married?"
She replied: "Due to the scandalously blessed Islamic revolution.
I am a drug addict, a self-selling, and accept cash only."

601. The first twenty years of my life passed like a wind.
And the December of my life passed like the month of July.
On the twenty-second day in the August of 2001,
Seeking more truths, I passed the age of seventy.

602. Why are you expecting to see the ray of light coming out of mullah's grave?
Have you lost your mind and sanity?
What blessing did he provide you while he was alive
That he will provide you while he is dead?

603. Hey . . . You, who have become a narcissistic egotist because of your wealth
And you adhere to mullaism, which makes you too apart from God,
If you are interested in finding out your final status,
Go and visit the gravesites of millionaires in a cemetery.

604. My Dear Friends: don't give your spouse a silence treatment.
Don't exaggerate her flaws; don't make a sea out of a creek.
The precious life is short and full of zigzags.
Don't make it bitter and poisonous for your spouse and children.

85: *Sirat Bridge:* A bridge that leads the Moslems to Hell or Heaven on the day of Resurrection.

605. Hey . . . You Mullahs: you are, indeed, sinful and shameless.
Don't tell me your logic is based on reality.
If you keep claiming you are reasonable and tolerant.
Then why, instead of reasoning, you behead your opponents?

606. The turban or the cloak is not the sign of genuine religiosity.
Wearing hats or bathing suits is not the sign of blasphemy.
There are many turban-wearing people who get drunk every night.
And there are many hat-wearing people who have never tasted alcohol.

607. There are many who laugh, but are tearful inside.
There are many who shed tears but are laughing within.
There are many black-skinned people who are cleaner than angels.
And there are many white-skinned people who are worse than Lucifer.

608. Hey . . . You Stupid Traitor and Unscrupulous Mullahs,
Your atrocities have surpassed those of Genghis.
You are more barbarous than he because
He killed people of other nations but you are killing your countrymen.

609. If you are the follower of the mullahs and their revolution,
Please listen to me, and realistically respond to this question:
Of their meaningless doctrine and their bloody revolution,
What have you gained except oppression, misguidance and insipid trait?

610. From whatever the sheikh has written and uttered
Nothing can be concluded, except ignorance, depression, and threats.
In a society where its leaders are Akhounds,
No one can go forward toward progression.

611. The mullahs have brainwashed you with superficiality and dogmatism.
Your pains are caused by their deceitful and pretentious thoughts and deeds.
Iran's weakness is what other countries wish for their exploitation.
But your lack of wisdom is the goal and hope of the mullahs.

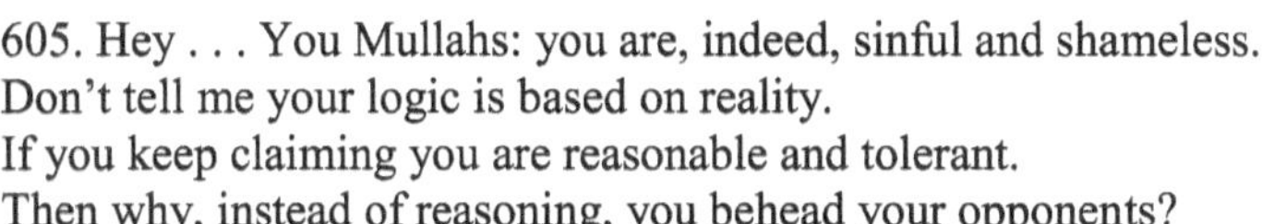

605. Hey . . . You Mullahs: you are, indeed, sinful and shameless.
Don't tell me your logic is based on reality.
If you keep claiming you are reasonable and tolerant.
Then why, instead of reasoning, you behead your opponents?

606. The turban or the cloak is not the sign of genuine religiosity.
Wearing hats or bathing suits is not the sign of blasphemy.
There are many turban-wearing people who get drunk every night.
And there are many hat-wearing people who have never tasted alcohol.

607. There are many who laugh, but are tearful inside.
There are many who shed tears but are laughing within.
There are many black-skinned people who are cleaner than angels.
And there are many white-skinned people who are worse than Lucifer.

608. Hey . . . You Stupid Traitor and Unscrupulous Mullahs,
Your atrocities have surpassed those of Genghis.
You are more barbarous than he because
He killed people of other nations but you are killing your countrymen.

609. If you are the follower of the mullahs and their revolution,
Please listen to me, and realistically respond to this question:
Of their meaningless doctrine and their bloody revolution,
What have you gained except oppression, misguidance and insipid trait?

610. From whatever the sheikh has written and uttered
Nothing can be concluded, except ignorance, depression, and threats.
In a society where its leaders are Akhounds,
No one can go forward toward progression.

611. The mullahs have brainwashed you with superficiality and dogmatism.
Your pains are caused by their deceitful and pretentious thoughts and deeds.
Iran's weakness is what other countries wish for their exploitation.
But your lack of wisdom is the goal and hope of the mullahs.

619. Hey . . . You, who are so proud to be an architect
And you are a teacher at a local college,
Why then during the past three years,
You have been postponing the repairing of your home's leaking roof?

620. Don't hurt your wife with your needling tongue.
Please do not degrade her in front of your children.
Never load the stresses of your job
On the tired shoulders of your devoted wife.

621. If you don't like America
And like Khomeini, you say: "Americans are world-eaters."
Then why for the purpose of getting your green card,
You are malingering and have seen three physicians?

622. Hey . . . You Iranian Lady: stand up with proud.
Avoid self-doubts, self-negligence, and idleness.
As an enticing stimulant of hearts, you are matchless.
Now it is the time for you to stimulate the brains.

623. Hey . . . You Man: when you will review your thoughts?
How long you want to deny your problems?
Your wife has confessed her difficulties.
When will you confess yours?

624. Hey . . . Iranians: who feel to be free from the king of kings (shah).
Alas: That you are now afflicted with oppression and religious primitivism.
Now, afraid of the truths and in favor of the mullahs,
You are drowned in the marsh of superstitions and illogical verses.

625. Hey . . . You little charlatan Akhounds,
You are misguided, debased and master of absurdity.
When, for the good and benefit of Iran,
You will be taken to hell by death angel?

626. Mullahs: your fasting is deceitful
Except human blood, what do you have in your cup?
I hope the day will come soon when
Iranians will push your wolfish snout in filthy mud.

627. Hey Sheikh: you are the one who is far away from God, not me.
You are the one who is hiding the Satan under your cloak, not me.
You are the enemy of mankind; but I am a philanthropist.
Thus, you are the one who should be afraid of God, not me.

628. Every country has its goodness and flaws.
And in its foundation, it has good and bad traditions.
Even though America has hundred flaws,
If you view it well, it has thousands of goodness.

629. Hey . . . Iranians: this leader of yours, whose insight is dim and polluted,
He needs to change his thoughts, sermons and conduct.
The criteria of civilization, in addition to progress in sciences and arts,
Are the freedom of thoughts, religion and Speech.

630. Hey . . . My friend: you and your spouse are not compatible.
You like rock and roll, but your spouse loves the classics.
For pleasure, you drink alcoholic beverages,
But your spouse drinks apple juice.

631. Religion has been mullahs' alibi for brutality, regression and looting.
Only theocratic dictatorship is reaped out of what the mullahs sow.
The Mullaists are those who, due to their lack of contact with reality,
They waste their lives by following the commands of the mullahs.

632. Even though the wealth, figure, and beauty are important.
The true collaterals of a happy marriage are
Reciprocal respect, trust, sympathy, romance, support and
Cooperation, communication, sharing and commitment.

633. My Friend: do you know why you are sad and tearful?
Because: you are brainwashed with the superstitions of life after death.
What benefit people gained from the first appearance of Imam Mahdi
That you expect to earn from his second appearance?

634. Hey . . . You who are planning to get married,
You better treat your pathological narcissism first,
Then if you have wisdom, use it and ask yourself,
"Why do I need to get married?"

635. The mullahs not only reject your thoughts,
They earn profit from your feeblemindedness.
The Mullaist is the one, who limits her/his thoughts.
Within the pathologically restricted thought process of mullahs.

636. The mullah-ridden who recited the Quran.
And did not listen to me, and continued drinking.
He was accused of abusing his children.
While in jail, he tearfully kept asking me for help.

637. Although suicide-bombing has recently become customary.
But the heavenly benefit for the martyrs is a delusion.
Whoever, for whatever reason, commits suicide to murder others
Is, without a doubt, deprived of mental health.

638. Poems are gold coins, and the poet is a goldsmith.
The coppersmith is unable to recognize the gold.
Whoever does not understand the value of my poems,
Is either a Mullaist or lacks insight.

639. I love your heart-pleasing voice.
I adore your temperament and serene behavior.
Come on and sit next to me, so I can
Make you laugh with my meaningful and humorous poems.

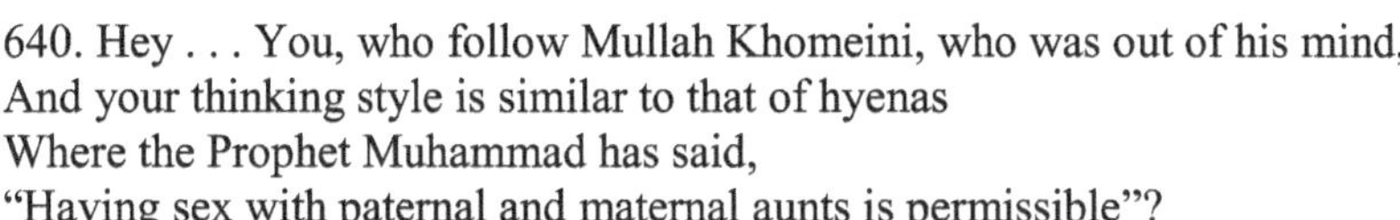

640. Hey . . . You, who follow Mullah Khomeini, who was out of his mind,
And your thinking style is similar to that of hyenas
Where the Prophet Muhammad has said,
"Having sex with paternal and maternal aunts is permissible"?

641. Hey . . . You Girl who live in Vanak, Iran,
And in the eyes of your mother, you are very gorgeous.
Please accept my apologies, because I truthfully think that
You are an old obese girl, who is spoiled and insipid.

642. I wish there were another world after this one,
And there were scientific record or evidence to prove its existence.
I wish after every century of living,
There was the possibility of returning to our youth.

643. Hey . . . You who, have not created even one poetic verse
And like an animal, you have been eating, sleeping, and using the bathrooms,
Why about the poetic style of Sa'ib Tabrizi, the Persian classical poet,
You are fruitlessly argumentative, crude and critical?

644. Hey . . . You who weigh three hundred and seventy pounds,
And like turtles, you are sluggish, lazy and slow.
Don't harshly criticize your wife's weight, which is,
Two hundred pounds less than your weight.

645. The Zoroastrian man who was a pathological gambler,
And, he never followed the pillars of his religion.
He did not listen to me, and after he lost hundred thousand dollars,
He killed himself last night in Las Vegas.

646. Hey . . . You, who are constantly fighting with your spouse.
And in front of your child you get drunk and dizzy,
Don't ever expect your child to turn out to be
The smartest student among his classmates.

647. Hey . . . My friend: I will not be pretentious like you.
I will not tolerate your doggish temperament.
If you don't adhere the principles of friendship,
I will never see you even for one moment.

648. Do you know why your son is depressed,
And he eats and sleeps less, and is lazy and pessimistic?
Because you hurt and abuse his mother
That is why you wife is so sad, disappointed and silent.

649. Hey . . . You Nonchalant Man who are addicted to alcohol
And for it you sold your home's furniture and carpets,
Don't deny your sickness.
Seek treatment while you have a chance.

650. Hey . . . You, who claim to be scientific-minded
And you have come to the US from Naeen, Iran.
Spousal and child abuse are felonies in this country.
Listen to me and "get off the Satan's donkey" (don't commit sin).

651. Do you know why your daughter is a narcissist
And believes no one is as beautiful as she is?
Because you have spoiled her to the extent that
She is lost in any other way except her own.

652. The water which is the essence of you and your foods.
Its purity and health are your responsibilities.
Don't pollute the earth because.
It will be your nest at the end of your life.

653. The Moslem who had no religious knowledge, but had a bushy beard,
His beard irritated and injured the face of his wife when he kissed her.
I advised him to shave off his whisker, so he would not hurt his wife.
He divorced his wife, but did not shave his beard.

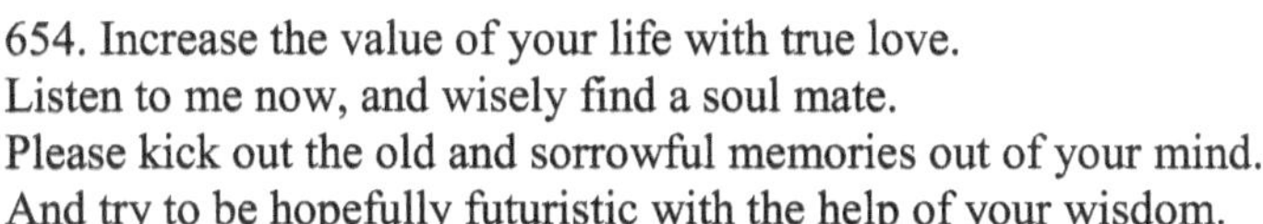

654. Increase the value of your life with true love.
Listen to me now, and wisely find a soul mate.
Please kick out the old and sorrowful memories out of your mind.
And try to be hopefully futuristic with the help of your wisdom.

655. If you are obese, find out how much you weigh
Then, try to decrease the fat in your body.
Instead of the poisonous drugs you are taking,
Exercise an hour a day before breakfast.

656. There are many alive, who are psychologically dead.
And they are also many who are deprived of wisdom and a true love.
There are many deceased who will never die spiritually.
Because: their souls are alive in their artistic and scientific legacies.

657. The man who was viewed by public as a good person,
But privately hurt the feelings of his wife.
I saw him while his wife was being buried.
He was sadly pouring the dust of her grave on his head.

658. There are many married couples, who are rich in wisdom and love.
And even though they are two bodies, but they are one in soul.
There are many physicians, professors, artists and theologians
Who have no knowledge of the art and science of true love.

659. Hey . . . Friend: make some effective attempts against your pains and sadness.
With your intelligence, realize the worth of your life.
If you want your life to be worthwhile,
At least do one good or valuable thing every day.

660. Hey . . . You, who is barking like a dog
And have lost your mental health,
If you don't want me to hospitalize you,
You better listen to me: take your medications regularly.

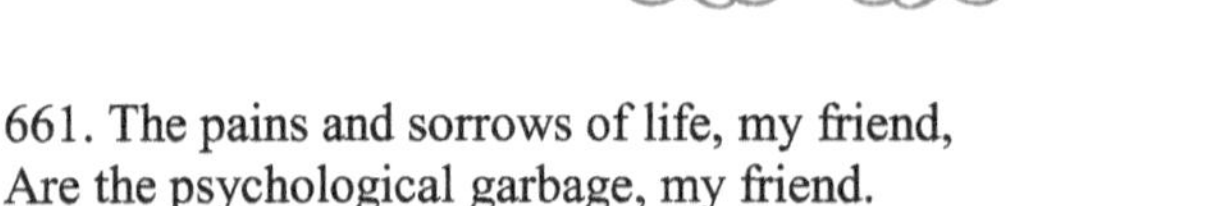

661. The pains and sorrows of life, my friend,
Are the psychological garbage, my friend.
With your intelligence throw the garbage out of your mind.
Are you a trash can my friend?

662. In earning your bread and water,
Use your own intelligence and assertiveness.
Instead of being envious toward others,
Compete with the ones who are ahead of you.

663. The religion which opposes to and denies the happiness of life,
It induces suicidal ideations in the souls of its followers.
The victims of religion are those who due to their ignorance and depression
Give away their lives for the sake of their religion.

664. I left this world to arrive in the alley of God.
Whoever seeks God never dies.
Hey you who pass my grave, don't ask how I am doing.
I was God's soul, thus I went to him (versed for my uncle's tombstone).

665. Those who take whatever you have in the name of religion
And disable you to fly toward knowledge by cutting your wings,
With the guilt feeling they have injected into your soul,
They make you depressed and disable for their own profits.

666. Those who claim they are practicing justice,
They use rascality in the name of God and religion.
Don't ever allow these ignorant and evil people
Have impact on or interfere with your life.

667. Hajjiah (female who has visited the Mecca) who was severely obsessive.
And she came to Newport Beach from Iraq.
She paid a high penalty and was jailed because
She stole shoes and handbags several times.

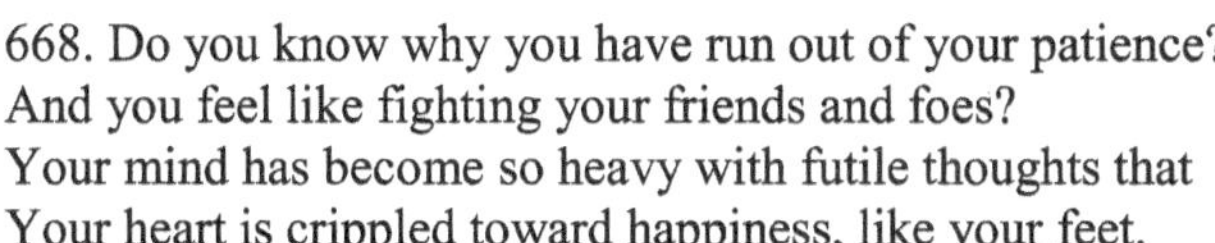

668. Do you know why you have run out of your patience?
And you feel like fighting your friends and foes?
Your mind has become so heavy with futile thoughts that
Your heart is crippled toward happiness, like your feet.

669. *Farkhoundeh*[86] who had beautiful face and figure.
And she worked in a tavern as waitress and stripper.
She told her father, who told her "You are a harlot."
"I am an artist not a whore, Dad."

670. Hey . . . My Friend: your cholesterol level is nine hundred.
It seems like your stomach has blocked your way toward treatment.
Don't eat two sheep's testicles with two fried eggs as breakfast.
Are you hurriedly aiming to get into your grave?

671. I wish the hereafter could be bright with the sun of justice
And there would be abacus and scale for measuring our deeds.
I wish instead of all the promised pleasures in paradise.
There would be possibilities for visiting our loved ones.

672. *Hashem*[87] who was not older than eighteen years,
And he fearfully kept satisfying himself by masturbation.
After he was punished by his mother, who saw him masturbating,
Shameful of his deed, he cut off his genitalia and died.

673. If you are planning to separate from your husband,
Don't feel guilty, ashamed and degraded.
Go and thank God for the fact that by this sick man,
You neither have a child nor are you pregnant.

674. The sheikh who has become the king and has enslaved you
And claims he is the representative of the Absent Imam (Mahdi),
While giving a sermon on Friday at the mosque, he said,
"Bleeding for God is permissible, but eating pig's meat is forbidden."

86: *Farkhoundeh:* Female name in Farsi language.

87: *Hashim:* Male name in Farsi and Arabic languages.

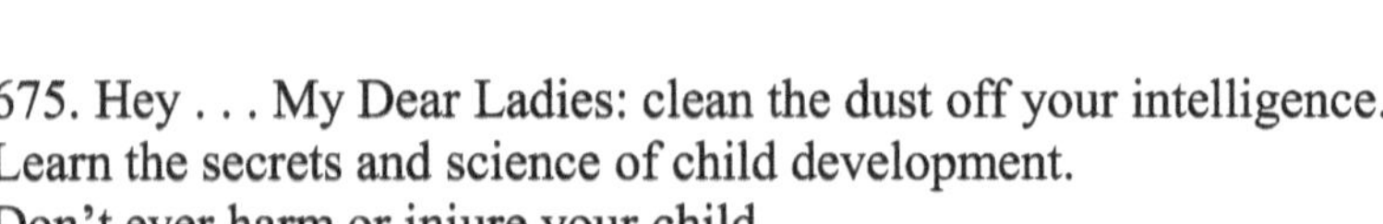

675. Hey . . . My Dear Ladies: clean the dust off your intelligence.
Learn the secrets and science of child development.
Don't ever harm or injure your child.
Never plant the seeds of superstitions in your child's personality.

676. Even though you have come out of the cave,
But still you act and think like the caveman.
Don't seek your goals with the help of the wells of *Jamkara'n*[88].
Have the mullahs fed you the *brain of donkey*[89]?

677. Give your heart to someone who is genuine in essence.
Seek your romance with emotional intelligence.
Avoid those who are unstable in temper and deed.
And they neither love you nor leave you.

678. Hey . . . You, who sell suitcases in the mall.
Do you know why your child is sad and tearful?
Be aware, if you abuse your spouse.
You are, automatically, abusing your child.

679. The severely phobic and depressed people
Are not insane; they have only psychological problems.
Mental disorders, like physical illnesses.
Have causes, courses and treatments.

680. The man who was a member of Iranian security organization
And afraid of the Akhounds, he fled to Denmark.
I heard from his brother-in-law that last night,
He committed suicide by prescribed medications.

88: Jamkaran: A small community near Qum, Iran, where there are two wells for males and females who, upon paying an amount of money, write their wishes on a piece of paper and throw it in the wells, where Imam Mahdi will receive it and make their wishes come true.

89: Brain of Donkey: an Iranian Proverb indicating that eating or being fed the brain of donkeys, decreases the level of intelligence of the eater to the donkey's level of intelligence.

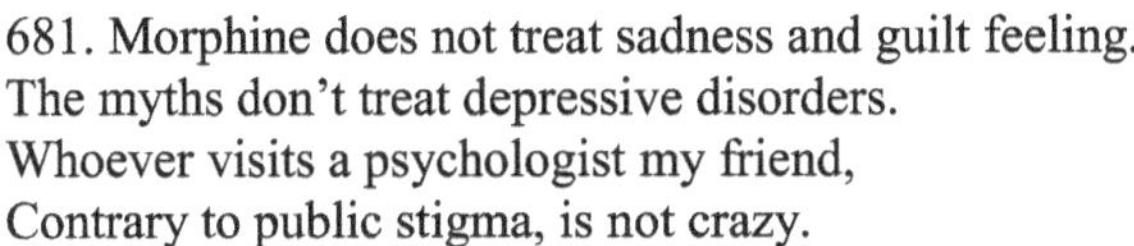

681. Morphine does not treat sadness and guilt feeling.
The myths don't treat depressive disorders.
Whoever visits a psychologist my friend,
Contrary to public stigma, is not crazy.

682. For how long you will be complaining of predestination?
When will you recognize your own flaws and mistakes?
For how long without freedom and human rights,
You will waste your precious life?

683. As long as you don't believe in the principles of determinism,
You will not be able to recognize the roots of your problems.
And if you don't find the roots of your difficulties,
You will never be successful in solving them.

684. Do you know why your husband is ill-hearted and cranky
And his brain is, like mullah's cortex, more chaotic than a pumpkin?
Please realize that the personality of everyone, whether normal or disturbed,
Is the product of a mixture of her/his genetic and environmental factors.

685. Our behavior, whether it is pious or evil
Is the manifestation of the method and content of our upbringing?
The mentality, perception and emotions of every one of us are
Like our foolishness and wisdom, indicative of our personality traits.

686. Bewitchment and prayers don't treat your grief,
Nor wine-drinking will treat your anguish.
Taking medications without having psychotherapy
Will not find and remove the causes of your depression.

687. Hey . . . You married couple who are both individualistic and stonehearted,
Don't fight and hurt each other like foes; since you are childless.
It is better for both of you to get separated, because
You are not at all compatible in characters and goals.

688. Hey . . . My Iranian Friends: your new ignorant President Ahmadinejad
Is neither civilized nor mentally healthy; he is not a humanist either.
What good did you gain from the former turbaned Mullah
That you expect to gain from this Akhoundeotic with no turban?

689. The repetition of "I love you" is although pleasant to hear,
But putting it into action, my friend, is much more important.
Your sympathy, respect, compassion, support and sharing are.
More effective than the medications your spouse is taking for depression

690. Hey . . . Mullahs: did you see the face of the Fake Imam on the moon?
And you believe that Mahdi, the Twelfth Imam, is on his way to help you?
Contrary to your long beard and idiotic sermons,
Your thoughts and insights are, indeed, short, distorted and pathological.

691. One hundred mullahs are not worth a hair thread of *Mossadegh's*[90].
Mullahs will never become a scientist like *Marie Curie*[91].
Whoever promotes and supports your ignorance and myth-worshiping.
Like Mullahs, will never assist you to progress toward modernity.

692. Hey . . . You, who elected Ahmadinejad as the president of Iran.
Why do you have animosity toward our country?
Do you know that, as your president,
He has destroyed the reputation of our country?

693. I went to see a friend whom I had not seen for years.
His wife said: "He passed away" while she began to shed tears.
I sadly asked her: "Where is his gravesite?" She said,
"We gave his ashes to the wind in the ocean by the piers."

90: Mossadegh, Mohammad (1882-1967): Iranian Prime Minister (1951-1953) during Shah's
reign, who nationalized the oil industry, which was under the control of Britih.

91: Curie, Marie (1867-1934): Polish-French chemist/physicist and inventor of radioactivity.
She received the Nobel Award twice.

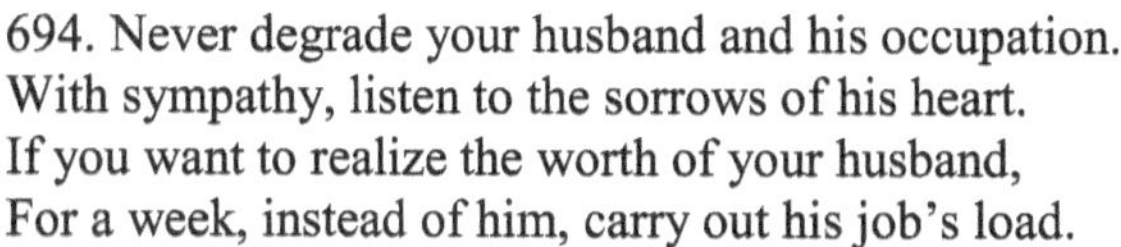

694. Never degrade your husband and his occupation.
With sympathy, listen to the sorrows of his heart.
If you want to realize the worth of your husband,
For a week, instead of him, carry out his job's load.

695. Hey you who, only by name, are Ahmadinejad,
But in essence, you are immature and heretic,
From which hole under the rock of ignorance,
Uninformed of the truth, you crawled out?

696. Hey President Bush: democracy is not a tractor.
The candleholder is not the place to install electric meter.
Don't export the load of democracy.
The goats are not capable of carrying the camel's load.

697. Hey Ahmadinejad, who are in charge of running our country (Iran)?
Without a doubt, your thought process is afflicted with a disease.
Your denial of Holocaust is exactly similar to denying
The unforgettable massacre in Kerbela

698. Hey . . . Lady: don't insult your daughter-in-law.
Don't add to her load of sorrows with your sarcastic comments.
If you want your son to feel good and be happy,
Don't make him suspicious and pessimistic toward his wife.

699. Hey . . . Iranians Americans: Let us believe in the principles of intelligence.
And while out of our own country, be nice and kind toward each other.
And instead of hating and slandering each other, or lacking harmony,
Let us, as a solid group, seek for the solution of our problems.

700. Hey . . . My Friends: marry someone who is seventy-five percent
Harmonious and compatible with you nature.
Don't ever marry someone who is only physically attractive,
But, she/he wants to marry you just for your wealth.

Index of First Lines

D

Did you see how the mullah threw the shah out of his kingdom? 38
Does everyone who has a good figure and is beautiful or handsome, 88
Don't assume that whoever wears a turban, 85
Don't belittle your worth by bending your head, 26
Don't ever develop friendship with Akhounds, 69
Don't ever expect absolute happiness in your life, 31
Don't ever give your friend anything except help and happiness, 44
Don't ever seek appeasement from the Akhounds, 89
Don't hoard food in your body my friend, 84
Don't hurt your wife with your needling tongue, 92
Don't lie and tell me you believe in the monotheistic books, 74
Don't listen to those who are sweet talkers, 46
Don't marry a man who is spiritually void but has a lot of money, 8
Do you know how fast life passes by? 43
Do you know how you came into existence as a man, not as a brute, 8
Do you know why happiness has left our hearts, 63
Do you know why I don't like the West? 24
Do you know why I keep praying to the galaxies, 24
Do you know why mullahs' mules are stuck in the deep mud? 89
Do you know why the laughter has left your lips? 31
Do you know why the mullahs are brutal? 16
Do you know why you are idle and shortsighted? 59
Do you know why you are not called a jewel? 26
Do you know why you are poor and sorrowful, 70
Do you know why you have become depressed, 88
Do you know why you have become frail and flimsy? 59
Do you know why you have many problems and sorrows, 70
Do you know why you have run out of your patience? 99
Do you know why your daughter is a narcissist, 97
Do you know why your difficulties don't become simple, 72
Do you know why your husband is ill-hearted and cranky, 101
Do you know why your son is depressed, 96
Do you know why your sorrows don't decrease, 74
Due to the ignorance that mullahs have hoarded in your brain, 66

E

Even though the wealth, figure, and beauty are important, 94
Even though you have come out of the cave, 100
Even though your coins of gold are more than the desert sands, 54
Everybody who visits the Mecca is not faithful to God, 66
Every country has its goodness and flaws, 93
Every mojtahed (jihad-ordering mullah) steals your mind and wealth, 81
Everyone who is born as a man would not become a human, 38
Everyone who is wealthy, well-dressed and good-looking, 44
Except tribulation, what have you received from the Akhounds? 59
Except you my dear, I don't have a beloved, 24

F

Farkhoundeh who had beautiful face and figure, 99
For a decade and half, we played the childish games, 41
For how long you will be complaining of predestination? 101
For many people, the Satan is the spiritual leader, 62
For some time, I moaned of the sorrows of love, 25
From the day the Arabs prevailed over us, 30
From the fire of true love, I am full of sparkles, 52
From the free-loading and unworthy Akhounds, 68
From the moment that Arabs crossed the boundary of our country, 76
From whatever the sheikh has written and uttered, 91

G

General X who, for the protection of our country (Iran), 43
Get up, come on, and let us leave this bondage to its pest, 7
Give your heart to someone who is genuine in essence, 100
God has blended the fragrance of jasmine in your clay, 9
Go on and pick up a flower, although it has thorns, 55

H

Hajjiah (female who has visited the Mecca) who was severely obsessive, 99
Hajji Ramadan, who came to the US from Saraab, Iran, 87
Happy are those who eat and drink their own bread and wine, 82
Happy are those who follow our creed and feel no hate, 11
Happy are those whose freedom is protected by their wisdom, 19
Hashem who was not older than eighteen years, 99
Have you ever read the Fake Imam's treaties, 32
Hey Ahmadinejad, who are in charge of running our country (Iran)? 103
Hey . . . Akhound: don't try to impose the narrations on me, 46
Hey . . . Akhounds: don't ransack the wealth of Iran, 76
Hey . . . Akhounds: God is angry and gloomy about your leadership style, 80
Hey . . . Akhounds: you are full of flaws in reality and wisdom, 54
Hey . . . Akhounds: you are impure in soul, and filthy from head to toe, 12
Hey Ayatollah Karroobi: you are, indeed, the source of deceptions, 79
Hey . . . Clergies: the proofs of your claimed honesty—we have never seen, 6
Hey . . . Dear Girl: I have not heard from you four years, 20
Hey . . . Dear Iranians: if you have zeal and ambition, 42
Hey . . . Dear Ladies: for nobody, you ever become slaves, 10
Hey . . . Dear Ladies: it is not the time to be intelligently sluggish, 17
Hey . . . Doctor: although your speech is very informative, 48
Hey . . . Friend: make some effective attempts against your pains and sadness, 98
Hey . . . Friends: don't let my laughter misleads you, 72
Hey . . . Girl: you are as cold and hard as ice, 13
Hey . . . Immigrants: if America is paying your expenses and feed you, 72
Hey . . . Iranian Islamic leader: you are more brutal than Zahaak, 33
Hey . . . Iranian Mullahs: you are superstitious and worship the intangibles, 58
Hey . . . Iranians Americans: Let us believe in the principles of intelligence, 103

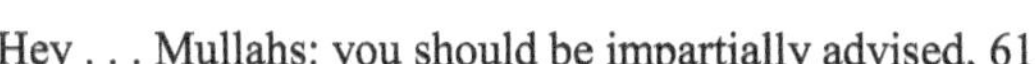

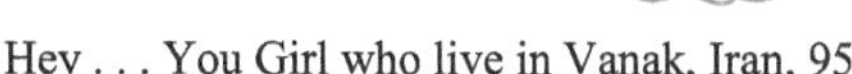

Hey . . . You Girl who live in Vanak, Iran, 95
Hey . . . You Girl who owe everything you own to your beauties, 47
Hey . . . You Girl who pressed my chest against yours so tight, 12
Hey . . . You Girl who shared my books, 18
Hey . . . You Girl: you have a lot of coyness, 19
Hey . . . You Girl: you have gorgeous figure and beautiful look, 12
Hey . . . You Gorgeous and well-mannered girl, 21
Hey . . . You impudent, malicious and foolish Imam, 42
Hey . . . You incompetent, unwise and heretic Islamic Leader, 42
Hey . . . you incompetent ayatollah who are misled and boastful, 48
Hey . . . You Iranian Ladies: don't dress up like Arab women, 77
Hey . . . You Iranian Lady: stand up with proud, 93
Hey . . . You Iranians: don't accuse the West of exploiting you, 72
Hey . . . You Iranians: don't allow the mullahs drown you in ignorance, 29
Hey . . . You Iranians: wake up and develop positive insight, 41
Hey . . . You Lady: who possess beauty, charm and charisma, 56
Hey . . . You late Fake Imam: you were certainly wicked and ignorant, 85
Hey . . . You Lazy Mullah, who were born out of wedlock, 71
Hey . . . You little charlatan Akhounds, 93
Hey . . . You Man, who go somewhere every night, 9
Hey . . . You Man: take a load off your wife's shoulders, 55
Hey . . . You Man: when you will review your thoughts? 93
Hey . . . You man who Committed Adultery, 73
Hey . . . You married couple who are both individualistic and stonehearted, 101
Hey . . . you Mean Sheikh: you are the true symbol of the devil, 83
Hey . . . You Mischievous Mullahs, 92
Hey . . . You Moslems: why do you believe in superstitions? 23
Hey . . . You Mullah: don't make your records more squalid, 40
Hey . . . You Mullah: don't think you are highly respectful, 60
Hey . . . You Mullah: for how long you talk nonsense? 25
Hey . . . You Mullah: neither you were born by God's will, 29
Hey you mullahs, who are severely deprived of arts, sciences and civility, 88
Hey . . . You Mullahs: don't broadcast the false news, 44
Hey . . . You Mullahs: If tavern is my temple, it is not your business, 27
Hey . . . You mullahs who live in Qum, 62
Hey . . . You Mullahs: you are, indeed, ignorant, debased and crazy, 28
Hey . . . You Mullahs: you are, indeed, sinful and shameless, 91
Hey . . . You Mullahs: you have no virtue, 85
Hey . . . You Mullah: when do you decide to take the path to the truth? 25
Hey . . . You Mullah: you are an imposter with rotten beliefs, 25
Hey . . . You Mullah: you are more vandal than Pharaoh, 35
Hey . . . You Mullah: you don't have the tiniest idea of the truth, 87
Hey . . . You Mullah: Your temper is like tiger's, 21
Hey . . . You Mullaists: take a good look at yourself, 58
Hey . . . You Mullaist: you are, indeed, misled and mentally disturbed, 54
Hey . . . You Mullaist: you are obese like a pig, 61
Hey . . . Young Iranian Generation: you are worthy of success, 52
Hey . . . You Nonchalant Man who are addicted to alcohol, 96
Hey . . . You Poets: don't write too many lyrics about romance, 35
Hey . . . You Prayer Leader: don't bend your body, 69

Hey . . . You President Mullah: your sermons lack total applicability, 49
Hey . . . You Priest who polluted the cross with your sins, 83
Hey . . . You Sheikhs: misleading the people is not teaching the true faith, 26
Hey . . . You Sheikh who are inflicted with scabs for years, 29
Hey . . . You stupid, blasphemous, and garrulous Akhounds, 82
Hey . . . You Stupid Traitor and Unscrupulous Mullahs, 91
Hey . . . You sullen and treacherous Army General, 66
Hey . . . You Superstitious, Moronic and Rigid-Minded Akhound, 68
Hey you Supreme Leader who, like a mule, are giving ride to Satan, 85
Hey . . . You Supreme Leader who are the flagman of Shiism, 37
Hey . . . You Supreme Leader: your sermons are void of truth and reality, 79
Hey . . . You supreme power: don't lie to and deceit people, 39
Hey . . . You talented, well-tempered, and expressive poet, 62
Hey . . . You the Fake Imam: you promised us a garden, 37
Hey . . . You the foes of our country (Iran): I hope you become parentless, 37
Hey . . . You the Iranian Revolutionary Leader, 35
Hey . . . You the professor in the science of genetics, 36
Hey . . . You traitor, hireling and deceitful Akhounds, 70
Hey . . . You tyrant and shameless mullah, 36
Hey . . . You: the victims of mullahs' collusions and secret deals, 57
Hey . . . You who, have not created even one poetic verse, 95
Hey you who, only by name, are Ahmadinejad, 103
Hey . . . You who are depressed and debased by mullahs' oppressive rules, 74
Hey . . . You who are planning to get married, 94
Hey . . . You who are poisoned by absurdities, dogmatism and superstitions, 45
Hey . . . You who believe in the intelligence of Mullah Khomeini, 79
Hey . . . You who complain against the deceitful sheikhs, 62
Hey . . . You: who complain of your pains and problems, 56
Hey . . . You who drink the ignorance the mullahs poured in your cup of life, 26
Hey . . . You who due to ignorance rip your chest with dragon, 86
Hey . . . You who gave our country to the Arab-ridden mullahs, 62
Hey . . . You who have, pains, suffering and distractions, 81
Hey You who have become spelled by the mullahs' bewitchment, 50
Hey . . . You who have robbed our country's wealth: I would not help you, 42
Hey . . . You who lead Prayers: don't do what the heathens do, 61
Hey . . . You who live next to the mosque, 68
Hey . . . You who only finished dabista'n (grade school): 81
Hey . . . You who sarcastically talk about our country, 46
Hey . . . You who saw the face of the mullah on the moon, 31
Hey . . . You who weigh three hundred and seventy pounds, 96
Hey . . . You woman who have a son-in-law, 64
Hey . . . You Woman: you are more sinful and filthy than the devil, 9
High bad cholesterol will not be treated by reciting the Holy Verses, 63
How long you keep sleeping with your seven-faced husband? 73

I

I adore your beautiful and questioning eyes, 82
I am lonely and sad in fighting with my heart, 18
I am the one who is kind to people, but receive no kindness, 16

I am thirty year old now, and seeking the secrets of mind, 17
I and my beloved were sipping wine and humming in moonlight, 7
I became romantically involved with a girl, 15
I don't know why I am so sad tonight, 65
If, as you claim: You are now healthy and intelligent? 46
If, as you keep saying, you don't like America, 73
If the mullahs start marketing prostitution under temporary marriage, 64
If you are complaining of your husband's temperament, 55
If you are happy or sad about the universe, 47
If you are in love with my looks and temperament, 82
If you are looking for your origin my friend, 18
If you are obese, find out how much you weigh, 97
If you are planning to separate from your husband, 99
If you are the follower of the mullahs and their revolution, 91
If you don't like America, 93
If you doubt the purity of the water you want to use, 41
If you have anguish, tears and fatigue, 81
If you have migraine headache or your fontanel lobe hurts, 85
If you have not read the poetry of Khayyam, 48
If you moan of the pains of kidney stone, 54
If you rationally view the Mullaists who are currently ruling our nation, 80
If you really and always think of God faithfully, 10
If your leader were not so rich in ignorance, 82
If your pains are more than your medicines, 64
If your patient sighs and moans of aches, 54
If your perceptions are reality-oriented, 74
If your wealth has reached the wealth of Qa'aroon's (Croesus), 43
If you want to live a long healthy life, 86
I had a lot of nostalgia and loneliness last night, 17
I have many flames of anguish in my heart, 65
I have seen many flowers where the cacti grow, 26
I hope one of these nights our lips meet, with yours atop, 8
I hope you never get tied up with the cowards, 20
I left this world to arrive in the alley of God, 98
I love your heart-pleasing voice, 95
I love your honey-tasting lips, 92
I love your kind gazes, 92
I madly love your coquettish manners, you hear? 11
I met a beautiful Christian young lady in the church, 21
Increase the value of your life with true love, 97
In earning your bread and water, 98
In playing the games of life, I am not a looser, 77
In the rotation of the galaxies I see good and evil, 22
I saw a girl in a church who had beautiful curves and edges, 14
I saw a little blister on the smiling lip of my beloved, Miss——, 13
It is winter and the chilliness is intolerable, 20
I went to see a friend whom I had not seen for years., 102
I will not follow the religion of the ridiculous priests, 89
I will not follow the superstitious deeds and sermons, 28
I wish mankind were free of discords and hostility, 87

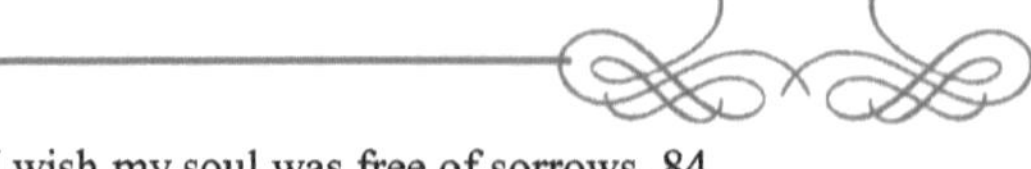

I wish my soul was free of sorrows, 84
I wish the hereafter could be bright with the sun of justice, 99
I wish there were another world after this one, 95
I wish wisdom was an international attribute, 83

K

Khatami: I am asking you without any fears, 52

L

Last night my eyes shed blood for your sorrows, 15
Last night my sight, stealthily, from her neck, 19
Last night she gave me a cold and unkind look, 15
Listen to me friends: pledging your mind to the mullahs is wrong, 56

M

Many people are running toward God, 75
Masoummah 26 who was only nine years old, 27
Morphine does not treat sadness and guilt feeling, 101
Moses who became a prophet by the order of God, 74
Mullah: azan (calling for prayer) does not help scientific endeavors, 58
Mullahs' slipper are more dangerous than warrior's boots, 29
Mullahs: the women's anguish is caused by your debauchery and stupidity, 67
Mullahs: your fasting is deceitful, 93
Mullahs: your path is darker than the bottom of the deep well, 77
Mullah: you are more of a stranger to Iran than the East and the West, 88
My adorable beloved: I wish there were a next world, 84
My beloved: With your exception, my other desires have left my heart, 6
My Darling: since my heart is not satisfied with our romance, 13
My dear Countrymen: get realistic and don't be a dervish any more, 58
My Dear Friends: don't give your spouse a silence treatment, 90
My Dear Friends: don't support the vulgar Akhounds, 46
My Dear Iranians: how long do you want to be enslaved? 42
My dear Lili: since you took your trip, I have missed you terribly, 53
My Dear Wife: I will not trade one of your eyelashes for tons of women's hair, 48
My dear wife Lili: Be sure that loving you is my creed, 49
My Friend: do you know why you are sad and tearful? 94
My Friends: about the person who tries to deceive you, 40
My friends: don't fruitlessly moan about life's challenges, 60
My friends: I wish there were hell and paradise, 9
My Friends: the narrations of Kuleini are all fabricated, 39
My Friends: the beginning and the end of our lives are both here, 42
My heart is full of anguish and mourning pains, 41
My Iranian Friends: who has made you debased and frail? 58
My life passes through action; not just through talking, 67
My sadness is the effect of your mystic romance, 12

N

Neither my life passed by following the misleading Akhounds, 38
Never degrade your husband and his occupation, 103
No one will lovingly bow down before you like me, my dear lady, 16

O

Oh . . . Dear Iranians: how long should you be the slaves of the idiots? 48
Oh . . . Dear Iran: we should sacrifice our souls for you, 51
Oh . . . Dear Ladies: be alert and don't let the Akhounds abuse you, 51
Oh . . . Dear Lady: you are as beautiful as an angel, 47
Oh . . . God: be generous to my country (Iran), 71
Oh . . . God: be sure that man will never become angel-hearted, 19
Oh . . . God: don't make me feel fed up with life's pain, my master, 10
Oh . . . God: even though you turned off the life-light of my mother, 41
Oh . . . God: help me, and debase my non-appreciative foe, 41
Oh . . . God: I am indisposed; give me a chance to travel, 22
Oh . . . God: I am not asking you to do too many things, 30
Oh . . . God: if you help us fight and terminate mullahs' oppression, 38
Oh . . . God: I have a firing anguish in my heart, 55
Oh . . . God: in thanking you for Lili (my wife), I don't have enough words, 60
Oh . . . God: make my romance competitor forever miserable, 12
Oh . . . God: once in a while pay me a little attention, 22
Oh . . . God: please have mercy on my soul which is now torn, 13
Oh . . . God: please take my unhappy soul, 14
Oh . . . God: thank you for creating human, 65
Oh . . . God: when will we develop wisdom? 39
Oh . . . God: you have innumerable hajjis (those who went to Mecca), 63
Oh . . . God: you know I will never separate you from my soul, 40
Oh . . . God: You should not have taken the girl I loved, 23
Oh . . . Iran: earn back your might, power and dignity, 57
Oh . . . Iran: from the moment that the shah was forced to leave you, 32
Oh . . . Iran: how about what you were before, and what you are now? 29
Oh . . . Iranians: don't be deceived by another turban-wearing mullah, 44
Oh . . . Iranians: don't make the sorrows of my heart overflow, 77
Oh . . . Iranians: wake up from the dream of ignorance, 7
Oh . . . Iranians who have been deceived and duped by the mullahs, 63
Oh . . . Iranians: who is concerned about our nation, 68
Oh . . . Iran: It is impossible to completely describe your sorrows, 22
Oh . . . Iran: what authority or power do you have now? 48
Oh . . . Iran: your bright dawns are darkened by mullahs' smoky deceits, 69
Oh . . . Life: don't threaten me with death, 28
Oh . . . Life: I will not lean on you tightly, 24
Oh . . . My Beloved: without you my soul is not free of sadness, 16
Oh . . . My Dear: don't fill up your hearts with anguish by mistake, 54
Oh . . . My Dear Friends: don't fill up your heart with anguish, 45
Oh . . . My Dear Friends: don't sadden others with your vengeance, 25
Oh . . . My dear friends: if you have a bodily illness, 49
Oh . . . My Dear Iran: have the sheikhs brought you a severe grief? 31

Oh . . . My dear Iranians: don't add to or exacerbate your calamities, 67
Oh . . . My Dear Iran: since I have left your lovely soil, 32
Oh . . . My Dear Iran: when will you become self-sufficient? 72
Oh . . . My Dear Ladies: why do you listen to and get sad by the sexist? 9
Oh . . . My Dear Lady: I will fascinate you with my accomplishments, 20
Oh . . . My Dear Mother: if you are ill, I will sacrifice my soul for your health, 40
Oh . . . My Friend: Avoid irrational guilt feeling, 20
Oh . . . My Friend: don't laugh at my sorrowful mood, 13
Oh . . . My Friends: don't ask the Akhounds about scientific information, 20
Oh . . . My friends: don't get angry with the bitterness of the truth, 69
Oh. . . My Friends: don't intent to fight your enemy, 21
Oh . . . My Friends: the orbit and you are in debt to me, 46
Oh . . . My Friends: try to protect your territory and boundary, 82
Oh . . . My Friend: why you are so tearful at each night and every morning, 11
Oh . . . My Heart: for how long you are sad and in pain? 16
Oh . . . My heart: you will finally kill me with anguish, 14
Oh . . . My Mother: for me, you have been more precious than a crown, 11
Oh . . . Neighboring Girl: I beg you, please come by, 10
Oh . . . Our King: fear God and don't fight him, 14
Oh . . . Poets: how long you moan of the unkindness of your beloved? 45
Oh . . . You, the Essence of My Soul: are you my beloved or not? 19
Oh . . . You Girl: I'm sad because our intimacy did not come around, 24
Oh . . . You Girl: in the creative artistry of God, you are a masterpiece, 23
Oh . . . You Girl who are Cuddly and have a Nice Figure, 22
Oh . . . You Girl who are my Classmate, 19
Oh . . .You Girl: you are lovely, desirable and full of coyness, 9
Oh . . . You Iranians: don't forget your glorious history, 38
Oh . . . You Obese Mullah who sound like a mule, 7
Oh . . . You: the ointment of my grief, don't forget your promises, 20
Oh you whose wealth and creditability have been robbed by the mullahs, 87
One day I with my wealth, youth and looks, 47
One hundred mullahs are not worth a hair thread of Mossadegh's, 102
Our behavior, whether it is pious or evil, 101
Out of the profits that mullahs have gained by restricting your lives, 32

P

People, who against drinking alcohol, collect document, 10
People ask me: "Why" I "moan all day and night," 15
People who are in favor of modernity and novel ideas, 30
People who seemingly protect Islam, 30
People who suffer in the month of Muharram with grief and pain, 17
Please, don't listen to the palmist nor believe in horoscopy, 44
Poems are gold coins, and the poet is a goldsmith, 95
Prayers don't make the country run well like in era of Jam (Persian king), 58

R

Realism makes you free of your pains and sorrows, 78

Religion has been mullahs' alibi for brutality, regression and looting, 94
Religion is not the means by which you can be scientific, 63

S

She drank wine, got half-drunk and fell asleep on the lap of mine, 15
Since our country (Iran) has been sacrificed for the profits of Akhounds, 75
Sometimes, a smile is more stinging than an insult, 62

T

Tell me: With the exception of the wicked mullah, who is your foe? 36
Tell me you girl: why you are so sad, 13
The akhound, who due to your immaturity, has become your ruler, 79
The akhoundeotic military captain who lived in Qum, 80
The akhoundeotic person who was obese like an elephant, 71
The Akhounds never honestly narrate the truth, 58
The akhound who, in violation of Islamic law, was greedy, 71
The beauty of full moon reminds me of your color and face, 50
The beloved demurs for her lover, 61
The beloved girl, of whom the beauty of spring was envious, 16
The Christian mother who has done many good for her mankind, 77
The devout Moslem who killed the youths in defense of Islam, 36
The elderly who spent their youth playing sinful games, 13
The first twenty years of my life passed like a wind, 90
The girl I loved, and for whom I did care and long, 8
The gullible people who invested their hopes in Iranian Islamic revolution, 43
The ignorant hajji who was our neighbor, 27
The Iranian professor who had Mullaistic mentality, 73
The Iranian woman who wore the veil and was the symbol of modesty in Iran, 84
The Islamic leaders, whom you consider to be an ayatollahs, 31
The lady who was depressed of being apart from her husband, 88
The loyal royalist who never gossiped against the Shah, 35
The man who got drunk and severely wounded his wife, 73
The man who ran away from the odor of wine, 44
The man who supported the Shah, 31
The man who taught the principles of Shiism in Qum, 37
The man who was a member of Iranian security organization, 101
The man who was a merchant of turbans and cloaks, 83
The man who was financially destitute, 34
The man who was one of the Shah's ministers, 65
The man who was viewed by public as a good person, 97
The men who are suffering from inferiority complex, 29
The more beautiful a woman is, the more unwise she might be, 10
The Moslem who had no religious knowledge, but had a bushy beard, 97
The mullah, who is seriously against drinking and fornication, 25
The mullah, who recited Quran's verses over the corpses, 38
The mullah-ridden man who came to US from Zarand, Iran, 85
The mullah-ridden who recited the Quran, 95
The mullahs' goals are to make you feel guilty, afraid and mentally insecure, 90

The mullahs have brainwashed you with superficiality and dogmatism, 91
The mullahs make more mistakes than their Supreme Leader, 72
The mullahs not only benefit from your lack of knowledge, 39
The mullahs not only reject your thoughts, 94
The mullahs say: "On the first night in our graves," 68
The mullahs whose source of income was reciting over the corpse, 53
The mullah who asserts it is religiously sinful to drink wine, 8
The mullah who claims to have a holy halo around his skull, 71
The mullah who has sacrificed your human rights for religion, 34
The mullah who left for Mecca, but due to his illness, he arrived in Turkestan, 53
The mullah whose savagery is worse than the caveman's, 71
The Mullah who teaches chastity and purity lessons, 70
The mullah who writes falsified narrations, 45
The Mullaist Iranian who lives in the West, 28
The Mullaist professor who taught physics, 80
The Mullaists, who for the fall of Shah, 30
The Mullaist who had no respect for medical sciences, 78
The Mullaist who has become the Iranian minister of guidance, 52
The Mullaist who never tasted the wine, 73
The . . . Mullaist who owns six rented houses, 81
The Mullaist who was a perfumer during shah's reign, 33
The nation (Iran) is now more heartsick than in Shah's era, 81
The nun who was obsessively addicted to prayers, 77
The Nun who was pure like the Holy Book, 76
The one who had not tamed his animalistic soul, 48
The pains and sorrows of life, my friend, 98
The people who claim they have created wonders, 32
The people who sound nice like nightingale, 45
The people who were vazeers (ministers) during Shah's era, 65
The person who complained of poverty and sorrows, 53
The pretty and unhappy woman who had no lover or friend, 7
The priest who directed a church, 75
There are many alive, who are psychologically dead, 97
There are many flowers which are worse than cacti, 36
There are many heretics who are in heaven, 76
There are many judges who are more evil than the convicts, 44
There are many married couples, who are rich in wisdom and love, 97
There are many people who are more innocent than Imam Hussein, 70
There are many smiling people who are crying inside, 76
There are many who laugh, but are tearful inside, 91
There are many women who are superior to men, 76
There are some rabbis who are like mullahs, 73
There is a sheikh whose tongue is like the stinging tail of a scorpion, 49
The religion which opposes to and denies the happiness of life, 98
The repetition of "I love you" is although pleasant to hear, 102
The robber who brutally killed his wife in Hamadan, Iran, 68
The scientist who wore bowtie during the reign of the Shah, 34
The seekers of the truth doubt whatever the mullahs say and do, 74
The self-praising man who worshiped himself, 70
The severely phobic and depressed people, 100

The sheikh's son who worshiped the wine, 86
The sheikh who claims to be a religious jurisprudent, 55
The sheikh who has become the king and has enslaved you, 100
The sheikh who has faith in the invisibles, 86
The sheikh who has gone to Mecca 4 more than once, 7
The sheikh who has madly fallen in love with the Arabic creeds, 78
The sheikh who is a pimp and matchmaker, 27
The sheikh who is defending the principles of Islam, 51
The sheikh who leads the prayer in the mosque, 78
The sheikh who presents sermons against corruption and undercutting, 70
The sheikh who totally follows the God, 22
The sheikh who wears black cloak, 40
The true believer in God does not need to follow the mullahs, 40
The turban or the cloak is not the sign of genuine religiosity, 91
The water which is the essence of you and your foods, 97
The wealthy ones who wear golden attires, 52
The woman I used to love and adore, 6
The woman who changed her Arabic name into Persian name, 84
The woman who had a lot of grievances from her husband, 23
The woman whose color changes of shame when she sees an unknown man, 87
The woman who was heartbroken by her husband's meanness, 85
They tell me "drinking wine will reap evil," 17
They tell me my beloved is not a Moslem because, 21
The Zoroastrian man who was a pathological gambler, 96
Those Iranians who had many grievances from the Shah, 61
Those who, are oppressed by the tyranny of the mullahs, 79
Those who, revolted against the Shah, 50
Those who claim they are practicing justice, 98
Those who claim to protect Islam, 39
Those who have been governing our country after the Shah, 78
Those who only think of and take care of themselves, 52
Those who returned our country to the Arabic-minded mullahs, 30
Those who sacrificed our country for religion, 87
Those who sacrificed you for their own benefits, 85
Those who take whatever you have in the name of religion, 98
Tonight, I am ill because I am motherless, 41
Tonight, I am without pains and sorrows, 56
Try to justly obtain your share out of life, 83
Try to keep your genuine faith from getting distorted, 34

W

We should call God now through our genuine prayers, 60
What benefits do you earn from criticism and denial of modernity? 57
What would happen if you were mine? 7
When I sleep, I will see your lips, eyes, face and figure in my dreams, 24
When the soul gets melancholic, the body feels pain, 38
When the sun sets, the thoughts of you rush into my mind, 8
When will the seeds of wisdom be planted in human brains? 54
Whether you are gratified or dissatisfied in life, 18

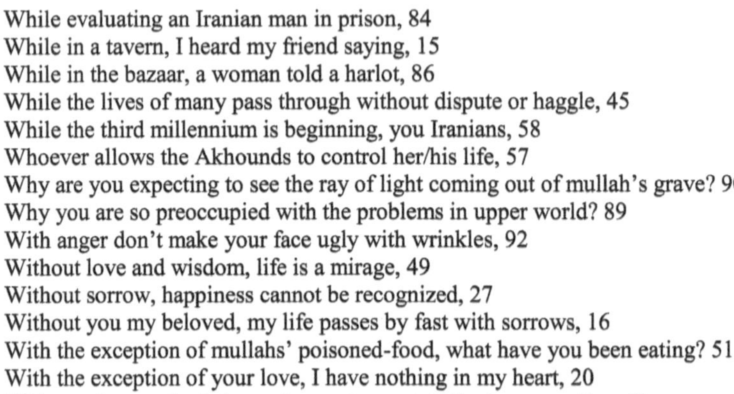

While evaluating an Iranian man in prison, 84
While in a tavern, I heard my friend saying, 15
While in the bazaar, a woman told a harlot, 86
While the lives of many pass through without dispute or haggle, 45
While the third millennium is beginning, you Iranians, 58
Whoever allows the Akhounds to control her/his life, 57
Why are you expecting to see the ray of light coming out of mullah's grave? 90
Why you are so preoccupied with the problems in upper world? 89
With anger don't make your face ugly with wrinkles, 92
Without love and wisdom, life is a mirage, 49
Without sorrow, happiness cannot be recognized, 27
Without you my beloved, my life passes by fast with sorrows, 16
With the exception of mullahs' poisoned-food, what have you been eating? 51
With the exception of your love, I have nothing in my heart, 20
With true love and wisdom, a home does not differ from paradise, 61

Y

You are my idol and except you I worship no one, 12
Your foresight is blind because the mullahs have polluted your mentality, 75

Z

Zahrah who fought for the women's right in Iran, 77

www.ingramcontent.com/pod-product-compliance
Lightning Source LLC
Chambersburg PA
CBHW021217130726

47988CB00002B/697